FABRICS

~ AND ~

WALLPAPERS

SOURCES, DESIGN
AND INSPIRATION

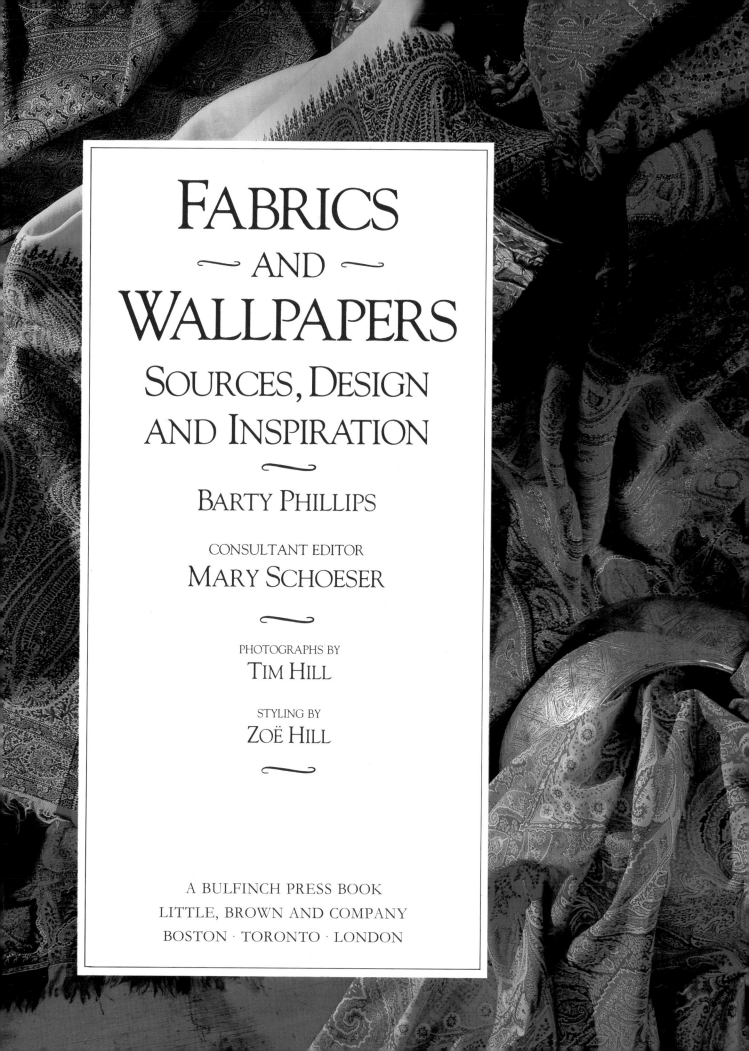

FABRICS
~ AND ~
WALLPAPERS
SOURCES, DESIGN
AND INSPIRATION

BARTY PHILLIPS

CONSULTANT EDITOR
MARY SCHOESER

PHOTOGRAPHS BY
TIM HILL

STYLING BY
ZOË HILL

A BULFINCH PRESS BOOK
LITTLE, BROWN AND COMPANY
BOSTON · TORONTO · LONDON

First published in Great Britain by Ebury Press, an imprint of the
Random Century Group, Random Century House, 20 Vauxhall
Bridge Road, London SW1V 2SA.

First North American Edition

ISBN 0-8212-1871-9
Library of Congress Catalog Card Number 91-57909
Library of Congress Cataloging-in-Publication information
is available.

COVER
"Sullivan" from the Chiltern Collection © 1990 Liberty of
London Prints Limited; PAGE 1: "Fresco" screen-printed textile by
Althea McNish for Cavendish Textiles; PAGES 2–3: nineteenth
century woven paisley shawls and printed fabric; PAGE 5:
"Mareld" cotton Jacquard weave by Barbro Peterson for
Kinnasand; PAGE 6: roller- and block-printed chinoiserie textile,
Mulhouse, France, mid-nineteenth century.

Bulfinch Press is an imprint and trademark of
Little, Brown and Company (Inc.)
Published simultaneously in Canada by
Little, Brown & Company (Canada) Limited

PRINTED IN ITALY

CONTENTS

FOREWORD

BY

Gill Saunders

CURATOR OF WALLPAPER COLLECTION
VICTORIA & ALBERT MUSEUM

Wallpaper has always been the poor relation in any history of interiors, and among the applied arts generally, despite the illustrious names associated with its design and development. By analysing patterns and their sources this book establishes clearly the mutual dependence of wallpapers and textiles. Pattern has always been an essential element of both, and, as we discover here, an enthusiasm for colour and ornament is shared by all ages and all cultures. This book takes a fresh and rewarding approach to the complex history of pattern: in place of the familiar chronological narrative organised by period or style, we have a richly illustrated analysis of generic types of pattern. This allows for illuminating contrasts between the design of disparate ages and cultures, and highlights the continuities of inspiration and influence.

The last two decades have seen an unprecedented interest in the furnishings of the past, especially fabrics and wallpapers. A concern with decorating interiors in a manner appropriate to the age and style of the building has created a thriving market for reproductions of historic designs, a concern that extends from the National Trust house to the Edwardian terrace. Accessible, informed, wide-ranging, this book will be an invaluable resource for the historian, the decorator and the designer, and indeed for everyone who takes pleasure in the infinite beauties of pattern.

INTRODUCTION

"Whatever you have in your rooms, think first of your
walls, for they are that which makes your house a home."

WILLIAM MORRIS (1834–1896)

The Victorian designer William Morris maintained that beautiful
surroundings improve the quality of life, and that of all the elements
which play a part in the overall style of an interior, textiles and
wallcoverings are among the most important.

Fabrics and wallpapers are not only crucial aspects of interior decoration,
they are also the most seductive of subjects for study. As the "clothes" of a
home, their designs and colourways are enormously interesting in their own
right, and they also offer fascinating clues to the way people lived at any
given period. From the magnificent tapestries of the Middle Ages, which
were transported around the countryside as part of the peripatetic life of their
owners, to the simple homespun cloths of the American settlers, textiles and
wallcoverings provide a mirror of civilization. Similarly, by following the
developments in weaving, dyeing and printing of textiles and wallpaper, it is
possible to trace the advancement of science and technology.

The history of textiles and wallpapers is enlivened by the larger-than-life
characters who people it. There was Jean Baptiste Réveillon, the Parisian
stationer who set up as a wallpaper manufacturer and produced papers of an
unsurpassed quality, until a revolutionary mob burned down his factory.
And there was John Baptist Jackson, the skilled English craftsman-designer

Traditional Navajo Indian patterns, such as this
"Eye Dazzler" rug, display the geometric motifs,
bold colours and apparent simplicity common to
many ethnic weaves. Only in the past 120 years
have such patterns begun to be incorporated into
Western fabric design.

who became so successful that nearly all fine wallpapers of the time were credited to him, whether he had been responsible for them or not. William Morris, generally thought of as a good-tempered teddybear figure, had an explosive temper; when he died, his physician said it was caused by "simply being William Morris and having done more than ten men".

Another rich vein in the history of textiles is provided by ethnic communities and tribes whose woven designs have hardly changed over the centuries, and are still very dependent upon local materials and on the type of loom used. Tribal weavers have produced work of the most exquisite skill. These weaves have come into their own today; both old and new textiles are highly saleable and have been the inspiration for many modern designs.

This is primarily a book about pattern, and it deals with specific types of pattern and their sources in some detail. The first three chapters of the book, however, cover the history of pattern in a wider perspective, to set the scene and provide a framework.

⌒ Texture, Colour and the Printed Pattern ⌒

The first chapter, Texture, looks at the textures and patterns produced by different types of woven fabric, examining weaving techniques and basic weave structures, looms and fibres, and, in particular, sources of inspiration from the past. We follow the history of woven pattern, from the figured silks of the ancient Far East, to the early woven textiles of Egypt, Persia and Italy. The Grand Tour finishes with the tapestries and woven silks of Flanders, France and Britain and the robust textiles woven in America.

Chapter Two, Colour, covers various aspects of colour, particularly the changing tastes in colour schemes and styles of Western interiors from the Middle Ages to the present. The chapter also looks at the effects of colour used in different combinations and with various textures. Finally, it examines dyes and their impact on textiles and wallpapers.

The third chapter, Printed Pattern, looks at the development of printed textiles and wallpapers and the effects on them of advancing technology. European textile printing—by hand, using wood blocks—was still fairly crude when Indian floral cottons were introduced to the West in the seventeenth century. The fabrics created great excitement, and it was not long before the French and English had begun to imitate the Indian techniques.

It was at about this time that wallpaper was transformed from a novel form of wall decoration, using simple black-and-white block prints, into a wallcovering that was in great demand. Printing techniques and the development of the industry roughly paralleled those of the textile industry, progressing steadily through the eighteenth century.

The nineteenth century suddenly erupted with change. New inventions in paper manufacture and printing meant that cloth and wallpapers could be

Damasks and brocades are among the most luxurious of fabrics. Here, a nineteenth-century striped silk damask (centre) and a nineteenth-century ecclesiastical brocade (bottom right) are surrounded by modern versions in cotton, linen-and-cotton, and silk. Wallpapers such as these "damask" patterns by Sanderson and Cole & Son echo the sumptuousness of the fabrics (details on page 194).

printed faster, making them accessible to more people. The hand blocking and copperplate printing of the eighteenth century were largely replaced by roller printing, and the first synthetic dyes were discovered, opening up exciting new possibilities in colour and design. In the 1950s and '60s screen printing made a great surge forward, when larger patterns became possible and different styles and ideas emerged. Today's screen printing is mainly done on rotary machines and is capable of very subtle, sophisticated designs.

⌒ Types of Pattern ⌒

The remainder of the book is about different types of design. Chapter Four, Abstract Pattern, covers patterns that are either completely abstract (such as geometric designs or splashes of colour) or semi-abstract. The long history of abstract pattern provided rich source material for later designers, from intricate Celtic knots to timeless ethnic weaves, from Gothic motifs derived from medieval church architecture to avant-garde patterns drawn from modern art. Similarly, the geometric shapes that were such a feature of Art Deco architecture, furniture and pottery in the 1920s and 1930s also dominated the textiles and wallpapers.

Chapter Five covers Stylized Pattern, which is taken to mean designs based on natural or known forms, in which the original forms have become secondary to the pattern as a whole. There are a multitude of these designs, from the Constructivist designs of post-Revolutionary Russia, with their rows of tiny tractors or sheaves of wheat, to the small sprigged wallpapers of Regency Britain. In many Art Nouveau fabrics and wallpapers, too, the colour, shape and general impact of the design were more important than any recognizable motif. The stylized motifs of Provençal prints and of paisleys have a fascinating history which began in India five hundred years ago.

Flora and Fauna, the subject of Chapter Six, speaks for itself. The first Indian cotton prints portrayed exquisite flowers, leaves, animals and birds, meticulously observed and painted. All through the ages plants and animals have been shown on fabrics and wallpapers. There was a time when British copies of Eastern floral patterns would combine different flowers on one stem and portray rather unlikely birds, but the Chinese and Indian patterns were always correct, down to the tiniest butterfly. William Morris too was scrupulous about botanical details for his patterns.

Chapter Seven, Pictorial Designs, includes wallpapers and textiles that are essentially realistic in style. They tend to emulate paintings, engravings or sculpture, often with *trompe l'oeil* effects, and depict a scene or story of some sort. Many pictorial wallpaper designs were vast and were intended to totally dominate a room. The hand-painted Chinese wallpapers which were so popular in the eighteenth century, and the French scenic papers of the nineteenth century, were designed to run around all four walls of a room,

The luxuriant bowers of this block-printed chintz manufactured in Mulhouse, France, in the 1850s, surround scenes inspired by painted wall panels of a century before.

forming a continuous panorama. Tapestries tended to be similarly large-scale. The famous *toiles de Jouy* were on a much more intimate scale but were traditionally used throughout a room.

⟳ Recent Developments ⟳

Today there is a greater choice of fabrics and wallpapers than ever before. Computerized Jacquard looms can produce almost any pattern; consequently, many designs intended for printing are woven instead. Modern printing methods, and in particular screen printing, offer great scope for both depth and subtlety in new designs. Yet historical fabrics and wallpapers are also extraordinarily popular today—and often the most successful are those employing the original dyes and production techniques.

This book can be used in several ways: as a good read for those interested in the history of patterns in interior design; as a sourcebook for those who want specific information on patterns; as a reference book for interior decorators or students; and as an inspiration for everyone.

CHAPTER ONE

TEXTURE

"The Ceres [Chinese] make precious garments
resembling in colour the flowers of the field and rivalling
in fineness the work of spiders."

DIONYSIUS PERIEGETES (AD 275–325)

Many of the patterns used in home textiles today take their inspiration from the woven patterns of early civilizations. In most woven textiles, pattern is an integral part of the weave rather than being printed on to the surface of the cloth. These fabrics are as pleasing for their texture as for their pattern.

Texture is inextricably linked to light and colour. Because some surfaces reflect more light than others, the same colour may look completely different on a flat or a rough surface. For instance, the intricate complexities of a single-coloured Jacquard weave rely entirely on texture to show the pattern; but when more colour is added and different types of yarn are mixed, the result is a shimmering interplay of colour, light, pattern and texture. The lavish woven velvets of Spain and Italy in the late Middle Ages relied very much on their texture to emphasize the pattern, and the intricate woven silks of China owed their exquisite luminosity as much to their porcelain-like surface as to their jewel-like colours. Ethnic weaves too derive much of their interest from the weavers' mastery of textural effects.

Many decisions have to be made by a weaver or designer when creating a textile, including the weaving technique and the type, thickness and quality of the yarn, all of which will affect the texture of the final product. The scale

A selection of antique and modern ikats: (clockwise
from top left) modern striped cotton from India
intertwined with an Indonesian scarf; silk ikat from
central Asia, c. 1890; modern wild-banana fibre mat
from the Philippines; modern cotton indigo
double-ikat from the Far East; striped silk ikat from
Persia, 19th century.

of the pattern is also important, since the larger the pattern, the greater the number of threads necessary and the more complex the apparatus required to lift the warp threads; small patterns, being cheaper to produce, are by far the most common. Yet another consideration is the fact that some yarns will accept dyes better than others. Wool takes dye very well and is thus available in a wide range of clear colours. Wool dyed a particular colour will not give the same effect as silk or cotton dyed with the same pigment.

⌐ The Weaving Technique ⌐

In weaving, one set of threads, the warp, is interlaced with another set, the weft, inserted at right angles. The loom keeps the warp threads under tension so that the weft threads can easily be carried through by the shuttle.

The simplest and most common of all weaves, the plain, or tabby, weave, is formed by interlacing warp threads and weft threads of equal weight and thickness. Canvas, taffeta and gingham are all examples of plain weaves. Other types of plain weave include poplin, in which a thicker weft gives a ribbed appearance, and rep, in which the rib is more pronounced than in poplin.

A second simple weave structure is twill, in which the warp and weft threads are interlaced in steps to form diagonal "twill lines" on the surface.

A third weave structure, satin, is similar to the twill weave, but with more random interlacings. The weft threads are almost hidden by the very fine, close-set warp, creating satin's characteristic glossy surface on one side, known as warp-faced satin.

The strong, reversible fabric known as double-cloth most often consists of two separate cloths, usually woven using plain weave but sometimes one of the other simple weave structures; each has its own warp and weft but they are interwoven to form one complete fabric. This is one of the oldest weaving techniques and is still much used today, mainly for bedcovers (particularly Welsh blankets) and wall hangings.

Plain, twill and satin weaves are uniform across the fabric, but some other fabrics contain a woven-in pattern. These may consist of simple geometrical repeats, such as the small diamond pattern known as diaper, or a combination of more than one weave structure, in which the contrasting textures create the pattern. In damask, for example, the glossy side of a satin weave is used for the ground, and the reverse, matt side of a satin weave (sateen) for the design. Damask may also contain other design details in twill or plain weave.

Fabrics like damask that combine weave structures are known as compound weaves. Damasks consist of only one or two colours, while multi-coloured compound weaves, or lampas, use extra warps and wefts in the patterned areas. Tissues, lisères and damasquettes are all types of lampas.

Another way of introducing colour and pattern is with short lengths of

Gingham is a plain-weave cotton fabric which originally was checked or striped. Today the term excludes stripes and conjures up fresh country kitchens, cafe curtains, and the informal chic of loose covers.

additional colour which are put in by small hand-held shuttles and allowed to "float" under the surface where not required. Brocade, for example, is a damask to which other colours—often gold or silver—have been applied using these "floating wefts". This technique creates an effect that resembles embroidery, as does tapestry weaving. In hand-woven tapestry, the pattern is wholly formed by the weft put in with the fingers and a bobbin or needle, the threads finishing at the end of the pattern instead of being carried from side to side of the work by shuttles. In machine-made tapestry, it is the weft that is hidden, with the multicoloured warp forming the pattern.

Pile fabrics are produced by creating loops during the weaving process, which are then either cut (as in velvets) or left intact (as in terry).

⌁ Types of Loom ⌁

Over the centuries, various types of simple loom have been used around the world. The early Egyptians, for example, used upright looms, while in medieval Europe most looms stretched the warp threads horizontally. Many ingenious ways have been devised for holding the threads in tension, from stretching them between the ends of a pliable stick to weighing them down

These three modern machine-woven tapestry fabrics are based on original hand-woven tapestries and are woven in France on Jacquard looms. Modern taste favours the rather sombre colours redolent of old tapestries. (From left to right) "Saumur" (abstract), "Chaumont" (floral) and "Blois" (stylized), all by Belinda Coote.

with stones. One of the oldest forms of loom, the backstrap loom, is constructed so that one end of the loom is attached to a tree or pole and the other is tied around the weaver's hips so that the tension is retained by the position of the body. All looms require a comb or reed to keep the warp threads evenly separated and an apparatus for lifting particular warp threads to allow the shuttle through.

The drawloom, originally developed by the Chinese, was the earliest type used for elaborate figured weavings. With this, the patterning mechanism was controlled by an assistant, the drawboy, standing at the side of the loom. Although the drawloom is still in use in China, elsewhere it was largely replaced by the Jacquard loom. This was perfected by the Frenchman, Joseph-Marie Jacquard, in 1801, though it was not introduced into Britain or America until the 1820s. A forerunner of the computer, the Jacquard loom used punched cards to control the pattern, enabling complicated figured fabrics to be woven. Today, sophisticated computer-aided versions of the Jacquard loom are generally employed to weave highly complex, richly patterned and coloured textiles.

Jacquard looms are used for damasks and other compound weaves. But weaves which have smaller overall patterns are still woven on a dobby loom, which was developed early in the nineteenth century; the resulting designs are sometimes known as dobbies. Plain, twill and satin weaves are woven on simple, or cam, looms.

⌒ Fibres, Yarns and Fabrics ⌒

Until the end of the nineteenth century, the fibres used for yarns woven into textiles were all from plants or animals. Cotton, wool, flax (spun into linen) and silk have proved to be the most satisfactory and are used today either on their own or in conjunction with each other or with man-made fibres. Man-made fibres include those which come from fibre-forming materials already existing in nature (notably rayon, or viscose, which is derived from the cellulose in wood pulp), and synthetic fibres (such as nylon and polyester) derived from fossil fuels.

With the obvious exception of silk, most of the classic textiles are named after their weave structure rather than the yarns from which they are made. Damasks, for instance, are traditionally woven from silk or linen, though wool or a mixture of yarns may be used. Tapestries are made from cotton, wool, worsted (a fine, smooth yarn spun from combed wool), linen or silk.

The finest and strongest of the natural fibres, silk has long been the most prized of cloths. Silk production was first developed by the Chinese around four thousand years ago; today, China and Japan are the world's main silk-producing countries, while the United States is the largest manufacturer of products made from silk.

Linen was first woven in Egypt, more than five thousand years ago. Linen and linen-wool mixtures, very fine and without pattern, have been found in ancient Egyptian tombs. Today, linen is still used in fine fabrics adding strength and character when blended with other fibres.

Cotton was first cultivated and woven into fabric in India around five thousand years ago. A very versatile fibre, it is still used in the production of most of the world's fabrics.

Wool was probably the first fibre ever used for textiles. Although it was not allowed into the temples by the ancient Egyptians, since they regarded it as being animal-based and unclean, it has been prized by most peoples for its warmth and versatility. Being soft to the touch, strong and resilient, pleasantly textured and easy to dye, it is used nowadays for the most upmarket weaves.

Medieval fabrics have names to conjure with. They included holosericum (made entirely of silk), subsericum (partly silk), examitum or samit (silk warp), ciclatoun (thin, glossy silk), sandal or cendal or sarcenet (a thin tissue of fine silk) and taffeta (thin silk for linings). Satin, camak or camoca (camel's hair and silk) was used as draperies on beds of state. Cloth of gold contained gold strands on their own or closely wrapped around linen, silk or cotton. (Silks and cottons from India, China, Cyprus and Sicily were often interwoven with gold and silver during the Middle Ages.) Baudekins, from Baghdad, was a fine silken shot cloth of gold which was spread overhead or behind the thrones of kings.

⌒ Sources of Inspiration ⌒

Textiles for the home reflect a number of influences—cultural, artistic, technological and fashionable—and few arts have been so inextricably associated with the industrial, social and religious life of people as that of weaving. Writers through the ages, such as Homer and Chaucer, have thought it relevant to describe the sumptuousness and significance of patterned fabrics of their time. The weavers of the Middle Ages had distinctive patterns, techniques and ways of using materials which have lasted over the centuries but have been interpreted in new ways. The origins of almost all pattern used in textiles had already been woven into fabrics by the time of the Renaissance. The early weavers were immensely skilled, and the detail and complexity of their designs have never been bettered. Though often created for clothes, these early textiles have been used ever since as a source of inspiration for furnishing fabrics and wallpapers.

The patterns of ancient and medieval weaves are clearly differentiated by racial and religious customs, yet Western textiles have been greatly influenced by Eastern tradition. This is partly the result of trading routes, and also partly because the Middle Eastern weavers were basically migratory, and

This red velvet cushion cover with the pattern in metallic thread and green velvet was woven in the seventeenth century in Turkey. Over the centuries Western textile designs have been greatly influenced by Middle Eastern patterns because the weavers were generally migratory.

The confronting lions in medallions, with other wild animals running between, were woven into this central Asian silk of the eighth or ninth century, demonstrating the type of motif that was introduced into Hindu art as a result of contact with Persia.

when they moved they took their weaving skills, techniques and patterns with them.

Many traditional designs woven by tribes and ethnic communities throughout the world have scarcely changed in pattern or technique to this day, yet have only in the twentieth century begun to have any real influence on Western design. Modern fabric designers, however, take these weaves very seriously—whether Indonesian ikats, Near Eastern kilims, African kente cloths or Peruvian tapestries (see pages 96–105)—and the patterns are beginning to appear in mass-produced fabrics, both weaves and prints.

Textile weaving probably developed from basket weaving in neolithic times. Many early weaves are remarkably beautiful and sophisticated, and the range of colours and patterns used is extremely wide.

⤳ Woven Designs from the Far East ⤳

Silk weaving is believed to have originated in China around 2000 BC. For centuries China produced nearly all the world's silk, which was the main factor in the opening up of trade routes to the West. Silks of the finest delicacy were woven in floral patterns of such sumptuousness that they preserved their distinctive character through many centuries and strongly influenced medieval European fabrics. Ornamental details were chosen for their symbolism. Signifying sovereignty, the seasons or good luck, there were floral emblems, dragons coiling through flowers, lotus flowers, tortoises (symbolizing long life), wild geese, clouds, butterflies and seaweed-like foliage. Chrysanthemums, peonies and camellias appeared frequently, and polygon shapes were used to enclose flowers and diagonal frets. The designs,

A fragment of silk woven in Persia under the Sassanian Dynasty in the sixth or seventh century. This "Senmurv", which was woven in repeat surrounded by heavy medallions, is typical of the mythical creatures which enliven many Sassanian silks.

which were richly woven together to create complex patterns look free but actually conform to strict conventions.

Like the Chinese, the early Japanese made good use of the indigenous flora and fauna, including the chrysanthemum, peony, iris, lily, bamboo, cherry and plum, as well as various birds, fish and dragons, all of which symbolized life or the seasons. They followed similar decorative conventions to the Chinese but with their own brand of spontaneous craftsmanship, accuracy of vision and clever techniques in representing the human body. The patterns often included hexagonal or honeycomb patterns and heraldic motifs.

The brief invasion of India by Alexander the Great in 327 BC introduced a Persian element into the native Hindu art. This was further developed by trade between Persia and India and also by the Arabian invasions of India in the eighth century AD. The Indian floral style reached a peak in the sixteenth century under the Mogul dynasty. The beautiful patterns of their woven cashmeres and printed cotton "muslins" included floral paisleys, richly brocaded with patterns taken from nature such as the pine, date, hom, iris and lotus. Other patterns included zigzags, wavy lines and tiny geometric shapes, all made up of small floral forms; and rosettes with grounds filled with small flowers. Symmetry and alternation played an important part.

Siamese woven textiles of the same period corresponded to Indian designs but depended more on the triangle and diagonal line.

⌒ Woven Designs from the Middle and Near East ⌒

Trading links are believed to have led to the spread of Chinese silk-weaving techniques to Persia (and from there to the West). By the sixth century, under the Sassanian Dynasty, the chief glory of Persian art was its woven silks. Including winged lions and other mythical creatures among the principal motifs, as well as horses, fawns, lambs, elephants and human figures, all within a wealth of pattern and colour, they were exported to Byzantium and also Europe and had a major influence on the art of the Middle Ages. Persian designs were characterized by a selective interpretation of their own flora, often set in a decorative landscape. Flowers included the pink, hyacinth, tulip, rose, iris and pomegranate; fish were common too. Trees were mainly the pine, date and cypress. An important feature of Middle Eastern design, the cypress was often used not only for its symbolism but also to give stability and "body" to the design.

The Greeks had their own traditions, of course. These mainly consisted of fret borders (the Greek key pattern) perhaps with rosettes or stars in very simple geometric patterns. With Greece being on the direct trading route between East and West, both Chinese and Persian influence appeared in textiles from around the sixth and seventh centuries. Greek fabrics might show, for example, Persian kings on horseback or hunting lions within the roundel (circular motif). Other designs might show dragons or Chinese-type ornament. Still others contained elephants inside enormous roundels with a symmetrical tree of life.

Roman walls were hung with tapestries and decorated with textiles. However, of the few Roman tapestries and other textiles that have survived, most came from Egypt, where they were probably produced. Silk was imported from China, and other textiles, including rugs, from the Near East.

The woven fabrics of ancient Egypt included cartouches, zigzags, lozenges, fret patterns, asters and small squares and other geometrics. The principal colours were red, blue and yellow with black and white. The lotus and tree of life were particularly common motifs. By around AD 300–700, the Copts (Egyptian Christians) had a highly developed weaving craft. Their tapestries, which were often made of linen and wool, and sometimes cotton, featured intricate small patterns including stylized birds, animals, foliage, vases and hearts; typical colours were red, green, yellow and purple. Figured silks showed roundels, containing single or symmetrically placed people or animals, such as lions, horses, fawns and parrots' heads.

During the first golden age of Byzantium, in the sixth century, looms were set up in the imperial palaces in Constantinople for the production of woven silks exclusively for the court. Decorative textiles of a high quality were common. Many were woven in circular medallion patterns containing flower motifs or figures and animals in horizontal or vertical bands. Typical colour combinations were gold and purple; red, gold and white; and red, green and dark blue. Another type of pattern had flowing ogival bands enclosing symmetrical pomegranate or floral motifs, with all the spaces completely

This fragment of Coptic linen has a nativity scene applied to it. The intricate embroidered design is enclosed in a medallion banded with floral motifs and hearts. The reds, greens and yellows are typical of Coptic fabrics from the fourth to the eighth century.

filled with small patterning. These designs spread throughout the Byzantine Empire and influenced fabrics for centuries to come.

⸺ Islamic Influences ⸺

For five centuries, during Europe's Dark Ages, Islam was the leading civilization of the world, having rapidly spread throughout the Near East, North Africa, Spain and Sicily. Saracen weavers had settled in Sicily and on the Italian mainland and produced a variety of rich silks and velvets. The most distinctive textiles were produced by weavers in the palace workshops at Palermo, Sicily from the early ninth century. The designs included animals, birds and foliage interwoven with inscriptions from the Koran or names of princes. Parrots, dogs, leopards, geese, lions, palm and date trees, eagles and swans, all symmetrically placed, made their appearance. There was considerable invention in the decorative quality of the designs. Intersecting lines or bands formed geometrical compartments within which birds or animals were symmetrically placed. Often, birds and animals in Cyprian gold, in which the thin metal was wrapped around a thread, were set off by a ground of crimson, olive or purple.

By the first half of the thirteenth century, much freer forms were being

Woven in the eleventh century, this Ottoman silk consists of large floral motifs banded with ogees. The ogee pattern was a distinctive feature of Islamic design and was introduced to Mediterranean countries by the spread of Islam.

This brocaded silk damask, woven in Italy during the second half of the seventeenth century, is typical of the rich colours, heavy use of gold, and large flowing designs for which Italian silks were renowned.

used, and figures were frequently introduced with heraldic motifs, animals, castles, rayed suns and trailing foliage.

Spain, too—under Moorish rule for six hundred years—produced textiles influenced by Islam, but with a complete absence of animals and flowers.

⌒ Italian Textiles ⌒

Italy's silk-weaving industry, established in the twelfth century, dominated the European market for over four hundred years. Most of the designs featured large patterns, particularly damasks or brocades. Florence and Lucca were famous for their superb figured silk velvets. Many of Lucca's silk weavers had come from the silk workshops at Palermo when Sicily was conquered by the French in 1266. Consequently, designs produced by the Lucchese weavers at this time were full of Middle Eastern imagery, such as pomegranates, birds, chained dogs, boats, swans, ducks, water, rabbits and ogival patterns; but vines also began to appear around this time.

When the Florentines conquered Lucca in 1315, many of the Sicilian weavers were taken to work in Florence, already a centre for weaving wools and velvets. They continued to use the symmetrical and radiating floral forms of Islamic textiles but abandoned the Islamic birds, animals and inscriptions. Bold, sweeping wavy lines, radiating flowers, and leaves within a cusp became the order of the day. At the end of the fifteenth century, during the Renaissance, vase motifs appeared in Italian textile design which reflected the new spirit of the age. By this time, Florence had become a major centre for silks as well as wools, and velvets and brocades were being produced in Genoa and Venice. Famous throughout Europe, the Italian coloured velvets were richly patterned with the pomegranate, Eastern artichoke and ogival patterns with gold and silver threads.

⌒ Flemish Weaves ⌒

The Flemish wool and tapestry crafts were established by the Emperor Charlemagne in the ninth century, and within a few centuries Belgium was noted throughout Europe for its textiles. Tapestry weaving was of particular importance during the Middle Ages and for several centuries to follow. Although demand for hand-woven tapestries was to decline dramatically during the 1700s, in sixteenth-century Belgium the industry was still thriving. It was at this time that tapestries began more and more to imitate the style of paintings (see page 183).

During the sixteenth century, Flanders was famous not only for its woollens but also for its silks and velvets and, most of all, for its fine linen damasks, which were highly fashionable at the time. Unlike silk damasks of the period, these linen damasks often had just one large pattern repeat, picturing biblical scenes, contemporary events, heraldic shields, Tudor roses, dragons and hounds, and later figures such as riders and huntsmen, as well as architecture and foliage. Smaller linens had patterns of flowers or emblems.

⌒ French Tapestries and Silks ⌒

The French silk-weaving industry began in the late fifteenth century. In the early sixteenth century, Italian and Flemish weavers were brought in to produce tapestries at Fontainebleau and silks at Lyon; by the mid-eighteenth century, Lyon had become the centre of silk production in Europe. Flemish weavers were also involved in tapestry weaving at the workshops in Aubusson and Gobelins.

Initially, the designs were based on Italian silks, but by the beginning of the eighteenth century the French were starting to use symmetrical forms of their own, gradually incorporating lace effects suggested by the early Italian laces and later the exquisite Chantilly, Valenciennes, Point d' Alençon and Argentan laces. The scallop decoration known as rocaille or shell work, which was so typical of Rococo patterning, was influenced by the work of Rouen potters. By the mid-1700s, delicate and graceful floral designs were becoming common. The Lyonese weaver Jean Revel introduced naturalistic flowers into French silk patterns. The distinguished late-eighteenth-century

French furnishing fabrics of the 18th century often used musical instruments and rural motifs as in this carving by Grinling Gibbons.

An elegant silk panel woven in Lyon, France, early in the nineteenth century. The paired swans enclosed in a medallion, the festoon and the border are typical French devices of the period. By this time the French had developed away from Italian designs and created a classical style of their own.

designer Philippe de La Salle—who specialized in large wallhangings and furnishing fabrics for European royal palaces and who was called the "Raphael of silk design"—made fashionable rustic and sentimental fancies, such as turtle-doves, shepherds' crooks, garden implements, interlocking rings and musical instruments.

With the approach of the French Revolution, there was a return to classical designs, encouraged by the discoveries at Herculaneum and Pompeii. Napoleon's chosen architects Charles Percier and P L Fontaine, who also designed interiors that influenced textiles, used Neoclassical motifs

such as medallions, lozenge-shaped panels, Grecian vases, acanthus, anthemion, laurel, palms and olives in sprays or festoons.

⌒ British Textiles ⌒

Medieval English textiles were mainly of wool and linen, but by the mid-
fifteenth century silk was being woven in London and Norwich. Flemish and
Dutch weavers played an important part in the development of the industry,
and in the late seventeenth century many French Huguenot refugees fled to
England (as well as Germany, Switzerland, the Netherlands and Ireland).
They settled in Canterbury, Norwich and, especially, the Spitalfields area of
London. Spitalfields became the main centre in Britain for silk damasks and
brocades, which were noted for the subtlety of their weaves and textures.

Emigré French Huguenots were also involved in establishing the linen
damask industry in Ireland at the same time.

⌒ North American Weaving ⌒

North American textile manufacture was based entirely on hand processes
until the early part of the nineteenth century. The majority of fabrics
produced were utilitarian, such as linsey-woolsey, a robust, warm fabric
made of linen and wool, the principle fibres of colonial America. Silk rearing
was attempted, and the first American silk factory was built in Mansfield,
Connecticut, in 1810. However, most silk cloth was imported, as were the
many other fine or elaborately patterned cloths that could not be locally
made. Damask was fashionable in America as well as England during the
eighteenth century. It was often woven with ornately Rococo patterns,
similar to Italian brocades of the late seventeenth century. Among the more
symmetrical patterns that remained popular were those with a basket of
flowers enclosed by ribbons and bowers, a style adopted from the French in
the 1760s.

Cotton was not an important crop until after 1794, by which time Eli
Whitney had perfected a method of stripping it away from its seeds by use of
a "gin". During most of the eighteenth century, cloths from Europe and
India were also obtainable in America, often arriving on British ships. Britain
discouraged the development of an American textile industry, but by the
1790s the first successful cotton spinning mill was in operation.

⌒ Weaving in the Modern World ⌒

Until the beginning of the nineteenth century, weaving was mainly done by
hand. But from about 1825 onwards, industrialization increasingly took over
the textile industry. The introduction of new technology transformed weaving irrevocably. The twentieth century has seen further great strides in the
sophistication of machines for weaving, so that nowadays almost anything is

Modern Jacquard looms can achieve virtually any effect, and modern weaves exploit this to the full, as in this design by Jack Lenor Larsen.

possible. This sophistication has, however, gone hand in hand with an appreciation of the skills of the early weavers and of the quality of the work they produced. In fact, much of the best modern weaving is an attempt to recreate in mass production the quality of texture and pattern found in hand weaving and to try to use man-made fibres to enhance traditional fabrics, rather than to supersede them.

It was during the 1920s and '30s that weavers began to appreciate the qualities of the man-made fibres then on the market. Rayon in particular was used to give a contrasting texture to natural fibres. In an experimental period that lasted well into the 1960s, explorations were made in Germany, Scandinavia, France, America and England, by weavers such as Anni Albers, Dorothy Liebes and Marianne Straub, who explored materials such as bamboo, mica, metal, fibreglass, cellophane and paper yarns, seeking new juxtapositions of textures and fibres. Designs too began to escape from the traditional and were boldly geometric or abstracted. After the Second World War they were often based on new science and technology rather than on recognizable patterns; the best known group of such designs was exhibited at the Festival of Britain in 1951 (see page 115).

⟶ Hard-wearing Fabrics ⟵

New sponsors of design came on to the scene after the First World War, as transportation networks expanded to include cars and later airplanes, which competed with trains and ocean liners. Many transportation lines turned to modern design to promote their service, among them London Transport,

who commissioned designs for moquette upholstery from Enid Marx. The brief was for something that would look fresh after hard wear without dazzling the passengers. The scale of the pattern repeat had to fit in with the economics of cutting the fabric for different-sized seats. The result was a range of designs in arrangements of formal geometric patterns in strong, contrasting tones.

Designs for utility furniture in the 1940s posed a new challenge to British weavers, and Enid Marx was again in the forefront with a range of small patterns, mostly stripes or geometrics, which would be long-wearing, aesthetically pleasing and economical to use.

During the 1970s the Welsh double-weaving industry, the colourways of which had remained unchanged for decades, was given a facelift by the British weaver Ann Sutton. She designed a range of bright, clear colours to bring these intricate, warm weaves back to life and make them compatible with modern tastes. Nowadays there are various different approaches to double-weave. Heinz Roentgen in Germany and several Swedish designers, for example, design double-cloths that are sometimes padded between the layers to give a quilted look. Double-cloths are usually of plain weave, but the Swedish designers Anna Severinsson and Barbro Peterson have designed double-weaves in broken geometric stripes using several colour shades, both for Kinnasand of Sweden.

⟶ Modern Patterned Weaves ⟵

There is a growing taste for pattern in weave again. Today's Jacquard looms make possible the most complex woven patterns, often combining as many as six to eight sets of coloured warps with two or more wefts. Large repeats and many different textures are possible, and further pattern is sometimes added after weaving. Renata Weisz, of Germany, uses discharge screen printing (see page 72) over large woven plaids; the unprinted plaid is available as a coordinate.

Modern Jacquard designs take their inspiration from a wealth of different sources. They range from intricate coloured abstracts produced by Aste in Germany and based on the colours used by particular painters, such as Gauguin and Dali, to a rich red and gold cotton viscose brocade produced by Brunschwig & Fils in the United States and inspired by Japanese obis (sashes worn with kimonos). Brunschwig & Fils also specialize in woven fabrics made to documented designs of previous periods, which are used to upholster their reproduction furniture. Hazel Siegel, of the United States, has designed a range of tapestry weaves based on original designs by the Dutch graphic artist M C Escher.

Some modern machine-made tapestry weaves for upholstery still rely on several sets of coloured warps that mix with several wefts to achieve many

Modern double-weave designs have come a long way from the traditional Welsh and Colonial American patterns. This vibrant Jacquard weave is by Barbro Peterson for Kinnasand of Sweden.

shaded tones. Others are weft brocades in which the weft appears to cover the warp completely. Jacquard frieze, or epinglé, in which only the warp is visible, has the potential for elaborate patterning, together with a carpet-like loop pile that makes it extremely hardwearing; strong natural fibres such as linen and worsted, sometimes in combination with cotton, are used.

⌒ Textural Variety ⌒

The polished finish of many fine modern damasks is partly due to man-made fibres. Marjatta Metsovaara of Finland and Anna Severinsson and Inger Högberg of Sweden may use Trevira, polyamide, viscose and wool, alone or in mixtures. Sometimes a tapestry weave may incorporate a chenille weft to achieve a contrast of texture. Man-made warp yarns are often used to create textural control. Docey Lewis, of the United States, uses soft, luxurious chenille fabrics with a velvety finish which may include mohair, wool, rayon, Lurex and nylon. Dana Romeis, also of the United States, designs damasks in rayon for Knoll Textiles. Manuel Canovas in France produces uniquely fresh floral damasks woven in rayon. Jack Lenor Larsen of the United States uses silks, wools and cottons but also enjoys using man-made fibres that do not imitate natural ones.

There is no effect that cannot now be achieved in commercial weaving. Inspiration comes from the most far-flung places and periods but also the times we live in—from modern cityscapes to new discoveries in science.

CHAPTER TWO

COLOUR

"The purest and most thoughtful minds
are those which love colour the most."

JOHN RUSKIN, *The Stones of Venice*, 1853

I n all ages, infinite pains have been taken to find the most pleasing
colours to decorate textiles and other surfaces in the home. Fabrics and
wallpapers are two of the elements which contribute most to the overall
look and are an easy way of setting the atmosphere and mood of a room.

Over the centuries, periods in which light colours were fashionable for
Western homes seem to alternate with periods of strong colour, and periods
of pattern to alternate with periods of plain blocks of colour. For instance,
European Rococo interiors of the eighteenth century featured greys and
pastels, whereas in the first half of the nineteenth century strong, heavy
colours predominated.

It is impossible to say with certainty exactly what colours were used at any
particular period in history. Fashions have always overlapped, and the
further back one looks, the less documentation exists. Experts disagree about
colours, and perfectly preserved colour schemes are rare. However, it is
possible to assess in general terms what fashions prevailed, and to examine
these wallpaper and fabric fashions in the context of the style of each period.

Textiles and Painted Colour

During the Middle Ages, contrary to popular belief, the homes of the
wealthy were full of colour, and textiles were particularly important. The
medieval home was cold and draughty, sparsely furnished and austere; it
relied upon colour to cheer up the spartan interior, and textiles to add a
degree of comfort. Walls were nearly always decorated, at the minimum with

Bright reds are associated with joy and happiness,
and there is no mistaking the cheerfulness of this
poppy-red fabric called "Clementina", produced by
Liberty in about 1900.

a simple coat of whitewash or colourwash, and often with painted designs such as red lines (in imitation of masonry), geometric patterns, heraldic emblems, roses or other floral motifs, or even large murals with narrative scenes. Green was the most fashionable colour, frequently embellished with gold. In the grandest homes tapestries were hung on the upper portion of the walls, while the reasonably prosperous made do with painted hangings of wool, worsted or linen. Textiles were also used on tables and as cushion covers. Favoured colours of the period were earthy reds, browns, ochre yellows, strong greens and deep blues, all obtained from natural dyes.

The grand homes of Elizabethan and Jacobean England in the late sixteenth and early seventeenth centuries were a riot of colour. The shades used by the wealthy were rich and vivid owing to the rare and costly pigments used, but those found in humbler homes were derived from the more common and subdued earth pigments. Only the finest wood was left undecorated. Wooden ceilings, wainscoting and timber chimneypieces might be extravagantly painted, sometimes in imitation of expensive materials or perhaps with geometric patterns and flowers. The first wallpapers appeared at around this time, in the form of separate panels (see page 74). As in the Middle Ages, tapestries were status symbols, and painted woollen and canvas imitations were common. The first piece of upholstered furniture appeared at the end of the Elizabethan era, in the form of the farthingale chair, which was covered in fabric leather, or turkeywork (using knots to imitate the effect of rugs from the Near East).

In seventeenth century England there was a tendency to cover the entire wall surface of main rooms, even in small homes, with wood panelling. Pale, honey-coloured oak had given way to pine by the beginning of the eighteenth century. Whereas the oak was merely waxed, the pine was always painted, often with a marbled finish or perhaps a wood-graining effect to look like oak, walnut or some other exotic wood, or sometimes simply in a pale colour. Any unpanelled walls were distempered white. Hangings of silk damask, brocatelle, wool or worsted, as well as tapestries, adorned the wealthiest homes. More modest houses had hangings of cheaper fabrics or even stencilled decorations imitating the fabrics in statelier homes, and the easily drawn pineapple was popular. Although not themselves inexpensive, wallpapers too were designed to imitate expensive textiles, panelling or marble. The growing taste for chinoiserie and Indian painted calicos (see pages 153 and 146) was apparent in the statelier homes.

⌒ From Theatricality to Simplicity ⌒

Europe's opulent Baroque style reached its apotheosis in France under Louis XIV in the seventeenth century. Rich, sombre colours, heavy forms and elaborate ornamentation characterized the style, but in the early eighteenth

From medieval times, the homes of the wealthy were graced with splendid tapestries and other hangings, such as this French sixteenth-century example. It is the central panel of a valance and shows an episode from the story of Lucretia.

century this gave way to the lighter, more frivolous Rococo style and clean colours of Louis XV. A Baroque style also developed in England during the Restoration and the reign of William and Mary, with elaborate wood carving, richly coloured tapestries and upholstery, Oriental lacquerwork and a heavy use of silver. The style reached North America about twenty years later.

England's Queen Anne style of the early eighteenth century (which spread to North America two decades later), followed by the early Georgian period, was a time of quiet elegance and simplicity. Panelling and other woodwork was painted, either to simulate high-quality woods or in muted colours such as olive green, brown, grey and off-white. The most common colours for printed fabrics were reds, browns, purples and black; bright printed fabrics were not widely available. Woven silks and velvets in crimson, green, blue and gold added richness.

⌒ Georgian Elegance ⌒

Eighteenth century English interiors were dominated by a return to Classical restraint. The balance and symmetry of Palladian architecture were keynotes of the interiors too. Decorative plasterwork had begun to replace wood

Brocades were extremely fashionable when this mid-eighteenth century silk, gold and silver example was woven in Spitalfields, London, then a major European centre for silk brocades, noted for their subtle effects.

panelling, but tapestry, velvet, brocade and damask were still popular as hangings. Curtains were becoming important for the first time. Strong colours, particularly crimson, green and blue, were used for interiors of the 1730s and '40s, but by the middle of the century paler colours such as bright pea green, sky blue and yellowish tints, along with "fine deep green" were in fashion. Chocolate was commonly used for doors, skirting boards and other internal woodwork. Matt finishes had replaced the eggshell-like sheen of paints used earlier in the eighteenth century. Elements of the Rococo style that was so popular in Europe crept in, and chinoiserie too was very fashionable. "China papers"—brilliantly coloured, hand-painted papers from the Far East (see page 186)—were the height of fashion, and European imitations were also produced (see page 153). Wallpapers, especially flock (see page 75), which imitated the expensive Genoa velvets (see page 26), became increasingly popular from this time.

In the 1770s and '80s, the main influence in English interiors was Robert Adam, who introduced a lighter, more elegant and harmonious form of Neoclassicism. Ceilings became more important and, along with walls, were often decorated with shallow, finely worked plaster ornaments, which were frequently picked out in white, against a richly coloured ground. Walls might be painted and decorated with a border, or hung with fabric, or papered. Neoclassical designers did not rely only on pastel colours; bright blues, greens, browns, lilacs and strong yellows were popular, and Adam's preferred colours are thought to have been blues, greens, yellows and reds (rather than pale blues, greens and pinks, as was previously believed). For the first time, window and upholstery fabrics, and sometimes fabrics on walls, either were the same or were at least in similar colours. This practice, associated with Adam, lasted well into the nineteenth century.

— Colonial Style —

In the American Colonies, a style that was uniquely American had developed by the beginning of the eighteenth century. Although styles fashionable in Europe, particularly England, influenced American design (sometimes after they had gone out of fashion in Europe), the American designers adapted and embellished them with great success. During the Colonial period—the period until the Revolution in 1776—paint was widely used, particularly in the form of stencilled designs, whether on furniture or, emulating rugs and wallpapers, on floors and plastered or panelled walls. Folk art motifs, such as the tulip, pineapple, willow, pomegranate, oak leaf, heart and log cabin, were popular. Wood was grained or marbled to simulate costlier timbers, or painted in strong colours. Blue-green combined with burnt sienna and yellow ochre was a traditional scheme. Other popular colours included blue-grey, oxblood red, bottle green and teal. Paints were homemade from milk and pigments and therefore had more of a sheen than the matt paints popular in England at the time. Block-printed and painted wallpapers, which were imported from Europe, especially England, were used in the main rooms, as were fabric wall hangings. "Toiles" (see page 174)—fabrics printed with Classical scenes and patterns, usually in a single colour on a white ground— began to be imported during the 1760s. In fact, some designs, particularly patriotic ones, were produced especially for the American market.

American flora and fauna were used in textiles as well as in stencil designs. As in England, plain-weave fabrics were spun and woven at home from linen, wool and, occasionally, cotton. The most widely used colour for this "homespun" was indigo blue (see pages 53 and 56). Most of the fashionably patterned furnishing fabrics were imported from England.

The Shaker communities, founded in 1774 and at their most populous in the first half of the nineteenth century, advocated light, simple, functional interiors. Chairs and household clutter were hung out of the way on rails, and the furniture, much of which was built-in, was unadorned, simple and beautifully proportioned. Walls and furniture were frequently painted in soft, cheerful reds, blues, greens or yellows.

⁓ The Federal Years ⁓

The American Federal period covers the early years of the new Republic, about 1780–1830. It was largely influenced by the Neoclassical style that had been popular in Europe for some time. Adam influences were noticeable but the style was more simply decorated than in England. Block printed wallpapers with Classical motifs were often used. Also, colourful scenic wallpapers (see page 188) were imported in huge quantities from France; depicting Classical scenery and stories and, from the end of the Federal period, American scenes, they were designed to be hung in sequence on all four walls of a room to form a continuous panorama.

Window treatments during this time became more formal, with restrained draped silk pelmets frequently used.

Towards the end of the Federal period, fashionable interiors adopted a more opulent air, inspired by the French Empire style that had been prevalent in Europe for some time, with heavier textiles and richer, more imposing decoration and furnishings.

This quickly developed into America's Greek Revival style of the 1830s and '40s, with its columns, pilasters, plain plastered walls, and motifs taken from ancient Greece, Rome and Egypt.

⁓ Classical Colour Schemes ⁓

Broadly speaking, Regency style prevailed in England from around 1790 to 1840. The key element, as with the Georgian period, was Neoclassicism, but with an emphasis on form and shape rather than ornament, and also with greater informality. Walls and ceilings were no longer heavily ornamented with plasterwork but often simply painted in a pale colour.

The general enthusiasm for Classicism was prompted in large part by the discoveries at Pompeii and Herculaneum in the mid-eighteenth century. Richly illustrated books about these finds, and also about the Acropolis at Athens and the temples at Paestum, caught the public's imagination. By the early 1800s, "Pompeian red"—a dusty, slightly brownish paint colour based on the deep reds of Greek vases (thought at the time to be Etruscan)—became popular for drawing rooms. Fashionable homes now had "Etruscan rooms", in which antique motifs were picked out in black and Pompeian red.

Favoured colour schemes were those that were supposed to have been

By the late eighteenth century the American market was a significant part of the European export trade. This wallpaper, featuring a corn motif, was produced in France specifically for the US market and was typical of the Neoclassical style popular during America's Federal period.

advocated by the ancients. For example, strong reds, blues, greens and yellows were frequently used alongside paler tints of their complementary colours. Sometimes they were also decorated with stencilled or painted black "antique" motifs.

Much of the interior woodwork, especially doors and window frames, was painted to imitate woodgrain, marble or bronze. Alternatively, it would have been painted in a colour—brown or green, not off-white as is often thought.

The fashion for uniformly painted surfaces coincided with the manufacture of readymixed paints, which at that time were always in flat, matt tones. The aspect of the less formal rooms was taken into account at this period when colour was chosen, and there is evidence that cool blues and greens were preferred for rooms facing south, whereas yellows, pinks and reds have all been found in north-wing attics.

Fabric was lavishly used in Regency interiors. Windows were elaborately decorated with a combination of blinds, curtains and draperies. The colours of the curtains were usually paler than the colour of the walls, and the blinds

were often blue or green or a lighter version of the colour used for the draperies. Textiles such as silk damask, glazed taffeta or wool were sometimes stretched over walls. However, elaborate brocaded silks were becoming less fashionable, and people were turning to plain satins, taffetas and damasks, and, increasingly, to printed calicoes. Slip covers in checked cotton or linen gingham, or sometimes printed cotton or chintz, were commonly used to protect expensive upholstery.

Among the printed furnishing cottons, pinks, reds, purples, browns and blacks—all based on the dye madder red (see page 53)—were the most common colours. Sometimes yellow and blue were also used. "Drab" shades (greens, browns, ambers) became fashionable around the turn of the century, and in the early nineteenth century buff, reddish orange, brown and Prussian blue, based on new dyes, were introduced. The taste for strong colours prevailed throughout this period's textiles, and motifs common during the period included pomegranates, grains, laurel wreaths, oak leaves, acorns, baskets of fruit and rose garlands. The so-called Regency stripe was actually a fashion of the 1950s.

During England's Regency period and America's Federal period, the

ABOVE: The first *toiles de Jouy* were produced in Jouy, France in 1770 and gave their name to this distinctive technique. Depicting detailed pictorial scenes, they were printed from engraved copper plates, normally in single colours on a light ground. These scenes by J B Huet were printed in Jouy c. 1790 using madder-red dye.

OVERLEAF: The discovery of synthetic dyes in the mid-nineteenth century caused great excitement, and the Victorians were lavish in their use of the new, bright colours available. The old and modern fabrics and wallpapers shown here (details on page 194) are typical of the Victorians' exuberant use of colour and pattern.

Empire style, which started in France in the 1790s, became fashionable all over Europe. As in England and America, this was a Classical period, but it was also influenced by Napoleon's military success in Egypt. Egyptian, Classical and patriotic motifs such as laurel wreaths, sphinxes, and the Napoleonic bee abounded in textiles. Walls were often draped with bright yellow, green or blue silk, to create a luxurious tented effect, and muslin curtains were capped with silk draperies. Many wallpapers imitated, or even matched, textiles, and the French scenic papers (see page 188) that were so successfully exported to America were equally popular in France.

⌐ Rich, Heavy Colour ⌐

In contrast to the Classical lines of the Regency period, the Victorians dressed their homes with a prodigious amount of "belongings" and, in terms of colour, a richer and heavier version of what had gone before. Dark red, bottle green, chocolate brown, maroon and deep glowing blue were predominant in a great profusion of pattern and ornament. The advent of mass production with the new printing machines and the Jacquard loom (see page 19) meant that people could use far greater quantities of fabric, draping it below mantels, across archways and doors, on tablecloths and over furniture. Heavy damasks might be covered by printed cottons coloured with the new synthetic dyes, often on black or brown grounds. These dyes—developed from 1856 onwards—added yellows, purples and bluish-greens to the range of textile colours available to the Victorians.

⌐ A Taste for Nostalgia ⌐

The Victorian period in England and America was characterized by revivals of a number of different historical styles, including Greek, Elizabethan, Renaissance, Rococo or Louis XV, and Gothic, all of which were freely interpreted and intermixed. For example, "Elizabethan-style" furniture, which was considered suitable for suburban villas and country houses, combined sixteenth century strapwork with Restoration spiral turning. Greek Revival was basically a heavier form of Neoclassicism. Neo-Renaissance style was characterized by heavy furniture, strapwork detail on textiles as well as furniture, and a colour scheme based on red and brownish-black. The curving lines, carved decoration and gilding of Neo-Rococo were regarded as ideal for drawing rooms, boudoirs and bedrooms. Gothic Revival was seen as suitable for dining rooms, libraries and billiard and smoking rooms. Its dark-stained wood, rich colour and medieval opulence made it one of the most visually exciting of all styles.

The Gothic Revival in America was grand and stately to an exaggerated degree. Draped hangings and curtains were lavishly hung over windows, beds, ceilings and walls. Ponderous colours such as maroon, dark green and a

brownish-black matched the general feeling of dignity. Velvets, velours and brocatelles were favoured for hangings because they gave a rich and luxurious effect. (They were being produced in America by the 1880s, which made them much less expensive than European imports.) Carpets might be paler, with highly formalized patterns in reds and pale blues. Both textiles and wallpapers often had stylized stonework, ironwork or "church window" patterns; red, blue and buff on a dark brown background were typical colours. Although incompatible in historical terms, opulent Rococo designs in moss greens and gold fitted well with the general "Gothic" mood.

⌒ Aesthetic Ideals ⌒

The Great Exhibition of 1851, held in London, proved a focal point for the reform movement advocating a rejection of much that was shown and a return to medieval designs and craftsmanship. Most closely associated with this movement are A W N Pugin and William Morris. About a decade later, the opening of Japanese ports to trade with the West, and the "discovery" of Japan at the International Exhibition of 1862 instigated a fashion for Japanese-style decoration. Melding together aspects of these two influences was the Aesthetic Movement of the 1860s and '70s, which believed in "art for art's sake". "Artistic" prints, weaves, and wallpapers were combined in interiors with exotic imports—some of which, such as Japanese "leather" papers (see page 137) and Near-Eastern kilims (see page 99), were imitated by European manufacturers. Arthur Liberty opened his shop in London's Regent Street in 1875; its Eastern Bazaar proved highly popular, and to these imports Liberty added English-designed "artistic" goods.

By the end of the century, much simpler, lighter colour schemes were common, relying on greys, greens and golds and fewer patterns. The most avant-garde households had lime-washed or panelled walls and polished floors with rugs. The general effect was a lightening of interiors, though respectable Victorian heaviness was not completely ousted. The idea was to choose neutral colours as a background, brightened by small patches of primary colour. Green was regarded as an Aesthetic colour, particularly a "warm apple green", which had been popular since the 1830s. Red flock had been fashionable early in the Victorian period, and reddish grey or Pompeian red was still considered suitable for late-Victorian dining rooms. Graining and marbling remained popular in spite of the Arts and Crafts movement's hatred of bogus effect. There was a steady growth of stencilling, too, but until the end of the century most of the decorative effects were achieved

Soon after it was founded, the London store Liberty's began selling
its own specially commissioned textiles, such as this design,
"Helmsley", from the 1890s.

through wallpapers and fabrics. A home writer in 1876 gave *Queen* magazine readers some precise colour guidance:

Hall and Staircase: sober yellowish drab and high red dado with two lines of white.

Dining Room: walls dark drab, with high dado of mauve and drab in alternate colours (curtains dark bluish green, bands of pale yellow and black velvet, embroidered peacock feathers).

Boudoir: pale blue, sage green, woodwork ebonized oak, wallpapers, ceiling lemon yellow, with apple leaves and nesting birds.

Drawing Room: deep maroon velvet, dark green walls, ceiling decorated with leaves and pomegranates. Woodwork black.

⌢ Natural Harmony ⌢

In reaction to the crude and violent purples, greens and reds resulting from the first synthetic dyes, William Morris led the Arts and Crafts movement of the 1870s and '80s back to the natural vegetable dyes of the Middle Ages for their wallpapers and chintzes. Morris believed that the colours of plant dyes harmonized naturally, that they were more permanent than synthetic dyes and that their restricted colour range would provide exactly the discipline necessary to restore high standards to design.

Morris advocated the use of what he called "frank red and blue", and his hand-woven wool furnishing fabrics of the 1880s relied to a large extent on those two colours. They were also the mainstays of his many-coloured printed cloths, which were softened by the paler shades of red, outlined with black and "made more tender by the additions of yellow in small quantities, mostly forming part of a brightish green, to make up the colouring of the old Persian prints which carry the eye as far as it can be carried".

The actual interiors could range from medieval baronial to the cottage look to elegantly Classical, but certain common features prevailed: limited areas of elaborate decoration, and contrast of plain and pattern. Typical colours were soft, earthy reds, greens, blues, blue-greens, old rose and dull gold. The light, spacious-looking, rustic rooms might have plain, pale walls, or tongue-and-groove panelling covering the walls to shoulder height, painted white or a pale colour. Or there might be a dado or a hand-painted or stencilled frieze. The walls might, alternatively, be papered in an Arts and Crafts wallpaper (see page 160). Window treatments were simple, and the oak furniture plain and upright.

Under the influence of Louis C. Tiffany, Candace Wheeler and their decorating firm Associated Artists, reform trends similar to England's Aesthetic and Arts and Crafts movements occurred in America at the end of the Victorian period.

Daisies adorned early Morris embroidery, wallpapers, carpets, and tiles. The predominant natural green in this design soon became a fashionable colour.

"Hera", Liberty's Art Nouveau peacock feather print by Arthur Silver, became the store's trademark. Liberty was so closely associated with Art Nouveau that in Italy the style was known as "Stile Liberty".

By the turn of the century the new synthetic dyes were being used with much greater subtlety. Art Nouveau was much less austere than Arts and Crafts. Although the style was never adopted as wholeheartedly in England or the United States as it was in Europe, Art Nouveau motifs and forms were apparent in textiles, wallpapers and ornaments (see page 129). Iridescent hues were used on pastel-dyed Japanese silks. The trend was typified by the famous peacock feather design (see page 168) commissioned by Liberty of London from the Silver Studio, a major London design studio.

A New Lightness

In the early part of the twentieth century, English interiors took on a lighter, airier, less cluttered look. Furniture was light and delicate, and walls—from which the dado was now absent, except in hallways—were pale. White or cream painted woodwork came into fashion, and the Edwardians experimented with the new high-gloss enamel paints. The main areas of walls and woodwork were treated with pastel shades, but ornaments and details were often picked out in bright colours; for example, black woodwork might be detailed with lines of aluminium silver paint.

The interiors of neo-Georgian architecture of this time—epitomized by the houses of Edwin Lutyens, England's leading architect of the period—were painted with pale creams and pastels, particularly quiet greens and blues—thought at the time to be the colours originally used by Robert Adam. (Lutyens himself, who often chose colours and furnishings for the

"Tiger Lily", an 1896 design for a printed fabric by the English designer L P Butterfield. It is typical of the controlled but sensuous lines of the English Art Nouveau style, which was an extension of the Arts and Crafts movement but more stylized.

buildings he designed, preferred much more daring colour schemes. He liked mouldings to be in white, to contrast with coves in black, a colour which he felt lent dignity and magnificence to a home. In his own home the drawing room had black walls with white woodwork and a green and white drag-painted floor, and it adjoined a red dining room.)

The English neo-Georgian style, with its tapestries and hand-woven silks, was also found in the wealthiest American homes, some of them designed by the influential American interior decorator Elsie de Wolfe, while a renewed interest in Colonial and Federal style was reflected in more modest U.S. interiors. Chintzes (see page 150) became very popular on both sides of the Atlantic, and a fashion emerged for matching floral fabrics and wallpapers.

⟶ Maintaining Neutrality ⟵

"Good taste" was a preoccupation of the 1920s and '30s. Interiors were simple and uncluttered, and, by the beginning of the 1930s, had few contrasting colours, relying instead on texture for decorative effect. An extreme example was decorator Syrie Maugham's all-white room scheme, which had considerable influence on interior design of the time. Syrie Maugham was the leading London exponent of the International style, or Modernism, which had emerged from the German Bauhaus. A design school founded by Walter Gropius in 1919, the Bauhaus advocated Functionalism—hard, glossy surfaces, metal tubing and plywood, white ceilings and walls, and a minimum of colour and ornament. However, the International style was slow to get established in Europe and it hardly affected America, until the school was closed in 1933 by Hitler, and Bauhaus disciples settled in Britain and the United States. As a result, in the mid-1930s young architects and designers, particularly in America, became increasingly influenced by the Bauhaus philosophy. Painters and sculptors like Ben Nicholson and Barbara Hepworth, who were producing abstract textile designs in the 1930s, were inspired by the wide range of differently spun and treated fibres becoming available at the time, partly as a result of work that had been done both in the weaving workshops at the Bauhaus in the late 1920s and in other workshops in England and Scandinavia.

Modernism remained a strong influence in Europe and America until the late 1950s. Nevertheless, the vast majority of people did not go to the extremes of the International style. The most commonly used colours in the 1920s and '30s were primrose, eau de nil, sage, and light neutrals such as cream, fawn, stone and buff. The few strong colours that were used were provided by Persian rugs and chintzes, which might have a rich red or maroon ground, and by colour accents like deep blue, coral and maroon. Graded schemes of, say, cream with brown, were considered smart, as were complementary schemes such as mauve with yellow.

Reflecting surfaces such as glass, silver and chrome were popular, along with metallic painting, stippling and mottling. British interior designer Betty Joel in a typical scheme combined silver walls and matt grey paintwork with grey-beige carpet, a coral and white rug and white silk upholstery.

Avant-garde interiors of the 1920s and '30s were decorated in a style that later became known as Art Deco (see page 113). The pale walls, painted or papered in shades of off-white or beige, created a sophisticated background for modern chrome, glass or leather furniture and exotic decoration. Even in more modest interiors, ornaments such as ceramics by Clarice Cliff and Jazz Age fabrics (see page 112) echoed the sharp oranges, lime greens and purples of the set designs of Diaghilev's touring group the Ballets Russes, which had created such excitement in Paris and London.

⌒ A Return to Colour ⌒

In the late 1930s there was a general move back to colour and pattern; in particular, bright yellow and orangey-pink, as well as black and browny-black, were used a great deal in textiles. By the 1950s most colour schemes were based on primary colours. The bright, clear colours and clean lines of Scandinavian fabrics (see page 118) typified the look.

In the 1960s and early '70s the preference for primaries changed to a passion for uninhibited "psychedelic" colours, mixed together in huge, swirling shapes. The mid-1970s inevitably brought a reaction, which led to brown as the basic colour and thence to greys and pastels. In the late 1980s

In 1990 the design team at Liberty of London Prints produced two prints based on the Art Deco designs of the 1930s, and specifically, but loosely, based on ceramic designs by Clarice Cliff and her contemporary Susie Cooper. The prints— "Melbourne" and "Cranbourne" from the Chiltern Range, which sell exclusively at Liberty in Regent Street, London—are shown here, along with some of Clarice Cliff's original pottery.

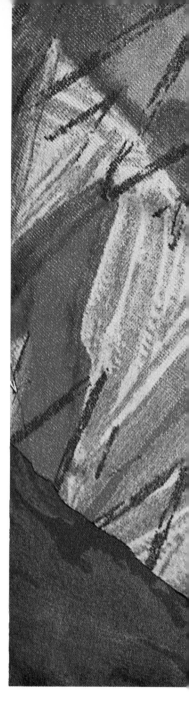

the mood continued, becoming gentler and more traditional. Small and large prints and florals of the cabbage rose kind, in fresh and pretty colours, were used against a background of various warm off-white colours, of which the most universally popular was magnolia.

Braver colours and more daring historical patterns—evident by the end of the 1980s—signalled the end of this quietly retrospective style. Neoclassical styles became popular once more, reinforced by the Bicentenary of the French Revolution in 1989. Eighteenth-century French patterns and Empire reds, greens and blues were very evident in the United States in particular. By the beginning of the 1990s many interiors combined deep, rich colours with Neoclassical motifs to create simple yet theatrical effects.

⌒ The Psychology of Colour ⌒

Colour in the ancient world was sacred. The Babylonians dyed the robes of high priests with red. Turquoise has always been the national colour of Persia (now Iran), used to ward off the evil eye.

Leonardo da Vinci related colours to the elements: yellow for earth, green for water, red for fire and blue for air. Nowadays colours are identified very specifically with mood. Deep blue is considered redolent of calm, silence, cold, melancholy and loneliness while pale blue is considered cool and refreshing. Reddish browns and russets are associated with warmth and cheer, bright reds with joy and happiness. Strong yellows, oranges and reds are said to be cheerful and stimulating.

In ancient times colour was used in the diagnosis of sickness, and yellow beryls were used to cure jaundice and loss of blood. Indeed there is some evidence that colour provokes not only a psychological but a physical response in people. Colour therapists believe that the varying densities of colours, created by their different wavelengths, have specific effects on the body's cells. Red is thought to raise the blood pressure, while vibrant colours in general, such as bright green and purple, are stimulating. Soft shades, on the other hand, are calming.

⌒ Sources of Colour ⌒

Fashions through the ages have depended not only on simple colour preferences, but on the dyes available and the effects that could be achieved. For example, the respect held by the Romans for Tyrenean or Phoenecian purple was partly due to its long-lasting, deep hue, but the high status it denoted resulted from the expense and scarcity of the dye, made from crushed mollusc shells.

Pigments for dyeing come from many sources. Safflower (*Carthamus tinctorius*) produces saffron yellows and reds. Turmeric comes from the rhizome of *Curcuma longa*, which produces a strong yellow but is not

Bright, vibrant colours are psychologically stimulating and were the *sine qua non* of 1960s designs. Trinidadian textile designer Althea McNish, working in England, created this abstract pattern for Courtaulds. Its zigzags and uninhibited colours were printed on silk.

colourfast. *Bixaa orellana* from Central and South America produces bright orange arnatto. Berberis produces yellow, Quercus (oak) dark brown, and Juglans (walnut) many different browns. The brilliant red of cochineal comes from Central American insects. Madder, a rich red dye obtained from the root of the Eurasian herbaceous perennial *Rubia tinctoria*, was the basis of many multicoloured prints until the nineteenth century; and indigo, important until the end of that century, is found in about fifty plants.

For centuries, the colours which were employed in distinct geographical areas varied according to skills and supplies. Many African and Indonesian fabrics are still produced in dark blue and nearly black because so many plants of the indigo-dye family are available there to produce this invaluable colour. India and China were the first countries to develop dyeing to a high degree, and early Indian dyers also used indigo, as well as madders, nutgalls, and blue and green vitriol.

During the Middle Ages and the early Renaissance, the dye industry spread from the eastern Mediterranean centres to the West. In medieval Europe many monasteries were known for the manufacture of sepia, made of the black-brown fluid from cuttlefish. By the fourteenth century, Florence was the most important city for the dyeing of luxurious fabrics and gradually once-specialized dyeing skills moved further northward. Woad, for instance, was the plant used for achieving blue in Europe until the seventeenth century, when Dutch and Portuguese traders began to import indigo from India. The Turkey red industry was established in the late 1740s in France and from there, in 1785, was transferred to Glasgow, where it remained an important Scottish industry until the 1920s, when the decline of the Colonial trade led to its demise.

The names of the colours we use today are often derived from the source of the colour or from plants of a similar colour. Thus in Britain, Turkey red was the name given to an especially fast, bright red produced from madder by means of a complex method originating in the Levant. The word azure comes from the Persian "Izhward", which means blue stone; mauve comes from "Malva" (mallow); purple from the rock "porphyria"; puce from the brownish-pink coloured belly of the "Pulex" flea. Ultramarine means "from across the sea", so-called because the lapis lazuli which was its source came across the sea from Persia, China and Tibet.

Right up until the 1860s the few hundred dyes in common use were derived from molluscs, insects and plants and were largely the same as those used in medieval times. Only with the development of mineral dyes (in the 1820s and '30s) and synthetic aniline dyes (in the 1850s and '60s) did the potential for colour change dramatically. After synthetic dyes (see page 56) were discovered and marketed to even the remotest parts of the world, they gradually took the place of natural dyes in many places. The Peruvians rejoiced in the bright oranges, turquoises and emeralds that synthetic dyes could produce, though there is now a swing back to natural dye colours there. However, there has been little change in many other places, such as Indonesia, where great significance is placed on the actual processes of dyeing using recipes handed down through generations.

It was William Morris who, in the late nineteenth century, in collaboration with Thomas Wardle (the most skilful British dyer of the time) revived the art of using vegetable dyes.

⌣ Types of Dye ⌣

The wide variety of dyes available today require different techniques, and many have been developed for use with certain fibres. Vegetable and other natural dyes are today associated with soft, warm colours while synthetic dyes are thought to be brighter, harsher and longer-lasting. In truth, natural

Modern dyes in this cotton Jacquard weave by Anna Severinsson for Kinnasand of Sweden equal the intensity once easily obtained only on silk and wool.

dyes can be very bright, but they fade (although many craftspeople prize precisely this quality, which results in muted, well-balanced shades). They are also harder to match, batch-after-batch, more costly to prepare and in some cases derived from scarce natural resources. So we rely on synthetic dyes (some of which are chemical "imitations" of natural dyes) to provide endless potential for richness of colour in the fabrics used in interiors.

There are several dye categories. Mordant or metallized dyes are by far the largest group, and contain both natural and synthesized dyes. Mordants are metal salts and are found as natural deposits in the ground, dissolved in mud or as soluble compounds in certain plants. They work by making a bond between the molecules of the fibre and the dye, so that strong and more or less permanent colours are produced from dye materials, which in the absence of a mordant would be pale or non-existent. There are several different ways of mordanting. Differently mordanted yarns (or areas in a print) can be put in the same pot of dye, and each will have a different colour, the various mordants having modified the colour in different ways. One of the oldest mordants, alum, made it possible to dye a whole range of permanent reds and yellows. Vinegar, citrus fruits, salt, stale urine and lye were all used as mordants. Many of the wood dyes were mordant dyes such as *Chlorophora tinctoria* (fustic), *Quercus velutina* (quercitron), Haematoxylon (logwood) and *Caesalpinia echinata* (brazil wood); madder root is the most important of this group. In 1868 two German chemists created a synthetic alizarine, the colouring matter of madder.

Substantive or "direct" dyes are groups of dyes made from flowers, roots, fruits and lichens, which dissolve in water and dye without the need for mordants or other additions. They are therefore the easiest to prepare and the least expensive to market. Lichens, known as "boiling water" dyes, are a good source of substantive dyes. Their colouring matter is in the form of colourless acids, and they need to be broken up or bruised and then boiled in water to produce colours. Untreated, they have no wash-fastness.

Coal tar dyes were the earliest true synthetic dyes. The first was discovered by accident in England in 1856 by W H Perkin. A bright purple which he called "mauvine", it made purple all the rage in fashionable circles for some years. Two years later R W Hoffman in Germany introduced the bluish-red known in English as magenta. Out of a flood of new dyes developed between 1860 and 1885, the ones that stood out were aniline black, methyl violet, malachite green and Congo red. There have been several breakthroughs in the production of synthetic dyes since the first coal tar dyes were discovered. Particularly important was the development of the first dyes that would "take" on man-made fibres. Among the latter are pigment colours, which are not technically dyes because they are soluble in water or in the solvents used for dyeing, so must be fixed by adhesive, resin or a bonding agent.

Vat dyes were developed from synthetic indigo, first introduced in 1897 and identical in structure to natural indigo, which has a natural fastness to light and water and needs no mordant to fix it. The preparation of natural indigo requires the leaves of the various indigo-bearing plants to be steeped in fermenting fruit, wood ash or stale urine for some days. The resulting mixture is pale yellow, and only when the cloth is dried in the air does oxygen cause the blue colour to appear. Vat dyes do not dissolve in water but are transformed into water-soluble compounds in an alkaline solution. During this process the oxygen is removed, allowing the dye to penetrate the fibres. The dye is fixed by subsequent oxidation. Used on vegetable fibres when excellent fastness is needed, vat dyes provide virtually any colour.

⟶ Colour Variations and Effects ⟵

Colours give a room individuality, and when enhanced by pattern and texture they clothe personal spaces by introducing sympathetic surfaces. As

Natural ingredients were used for many centuries to give permanent dyes which would not run but might fade over the years. The textiles shown here—which include a kalim kari bedspread, tablecloth and silk scarf; reproduction medieval fabric; Chinese tie-dyed fabric; Japanese kasuri fabric and Japanese batik—are all dyed with vegetable dyes (details on page 194).

Taffeta, with its high sheen and crisp texture, offers a marvellous opportunity for the sumptuous use of colour, in which light-and-shade and "shot" effects play an important part. The modern home-furnishing taffetas shown here come from Liberty (purple taffeta), Zimmer & Rohde (orange taffeta, top right) and Osborne & Little.

living spaces grow smaller and the opportunity for grand furniture and elbow room diminishes, people will come to rely more on fabrics and wallpapers to provide elegance, warmth, interest and dignity to their homes.

Whether a colour is seen as cool or warm, depends a great deal on the intensity and type of light, texture of the fabric and colour of the surfaces next to it. Pastels, which may look fresh and pretty in a clear northern light, often appear faded and grey in intense sunshine. Also, colours change perceptibly according to whether they are seen under natural daylight or artificial light. The bright, rich colours used in eighteenth century interiors seem surprising for such an elegant age, but, of course, they were seen in candlelight at night, and during the day were unlit except through the windows.

Even identical fibres dyed with the same pigments can look different if one has a rough or shaggy surface and the other is smooth. Equally, silk velvet projects colour differently than does cotton velvet or Dralon velvet, since each yarn has a different texture. Dark colours tend to look darker when hung at windows because of the contrast with bright sunlight. Velvets, nubbly weaves and other pile fabrics will appear darker than plain or satin weaves of the same shade. Damask, faille, brocade, velveteen and other rich textures are best in formal settings, which will emphasize the luxurious effect of their highlighted surfaces.

Just as colour can make a room appear warm and cozy or cool and spacious, so the mixture of patterned and plain surfaces can help to create specific moods. Red woven fabrics can give a great sense of comfort and well-being. The same colour on a shiny fabric can be exciting and stimulating, while with touches of gold it gives a subtly regal and sumptuous flavour to the room in which it is used.

Pattern and texture can set the style of a room in a way which colour by itself is unable to do. Whether the interior scheme is to be traditional or modern, elegant or ethnic, the combination of pattern, texture and colour will have to be compatible if the room is to achieve the desired ambience.

⌐ Colour Perception ⌐

Designers have had to cope with several unexpected problems related to colour. Every colour is made up of light waves of varying wavelengths, which vibrate at different rates. Placing contrasting colours, or cool and warm colours, next to each other can create distinct vibrations, making the pattern appear to dance. Striped or checked patterns with a strong colour intensity tend to vibrate too. To counteract this it may be necessary to change the proportion of light and dark colours, to lessen the degree of colour intensity, or to widen the stripes (wider stripes produce less vibration).

Another problem encountered by designers has been that of after-image.

During the eighteenth century, fabric printers found that a particular colour would often appear to change when translated from the small-scale original design to the larger scale of the printed fabric. A green pattern in a blue field might end up looking yellowish, black on red might appear green and so on, due to the influence of one colour on another. After-image effects were responsible for this phenomenon; the green pattern looked yellow because it contained orange, which is the after-image of blue; the black was tinged with the after-image of red, which is green.

The natural world is full of contrasts: of colour and tone, light and shade, rough and smooth, jagged and straight, geometric and flowing. Interior design requires contrasts too. Rich fabrics seem all the more luxurious when balanced by humbler ones, and a room furnished in only one period style can have a curiously "dead" quality. Modern technology has produced old and new designs on affordable fabrics which can hold their own next to the most magnificent textiles. Similarly, a satisfying variety can be gained by juxtaposing the colours and textures of machine-made cloths with the coarser textures and natural colours of ethnic rugs and hangings. Luxury fabrics are undeniably expensive. But the introduction of just a small amount of a sensitively coloured and textured designer material can alter the character of a room fundamentally. A hanging or a few cushions can make the difference between the merely pleasant and the unforgettable.

ABOVE: This design for a fabric printed in Mulhouse, France, in mid-nineteenth century, makes full use of vibrant colour contrasts made available by the then new synthetic dyes.

RIGHT: Textiles woven with gold have always been synonymous with luxury. This selection includes both antique and modern fabrics brocaded with gold, as well as modern gold-printed wallpapers (details on page 195).

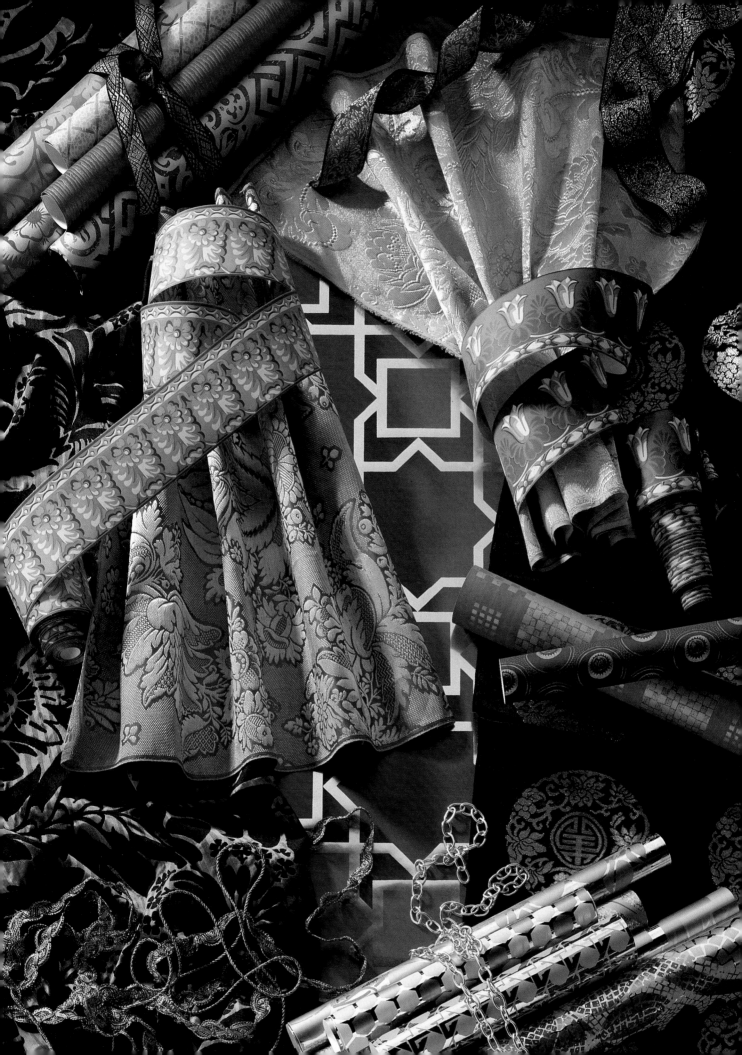

CHAPTER THREE

PRINTED PATTERN

"The machine will play an important part in the
advancement of public taste. Because of it the joy of pure
forms will be established again and again . . ."

SAMUEL BING,
proprietor of the Parisian shop, L'Art Nouveau, c. 1895

P rinting has been used to decorate fabric for at least one and a half
thousand years, but in the West the art of printing textiles and paper
hangings was perfected over the last two and a half centuries. Com-
pared to weaving, printing is a relatively quick and inexpensive way of
decorating a fabric and, with today's technology, is capable of accurate and
fine detailing.

The inspiration for printed designs comes from incredibly diverse sources,
ranging from Jacobean crewelwork to ceramics and woven baskets, from
Gothic cathedrals to Indian woven shawls, from flora and fauna to electronic
circuitry. And, of course, patterns have been copied, adapted or revived in
countless ways through the years.

Block-printed Fabrics

The earliest method of printing was block printing, which was first developed around the 4th century BC in the Far East. It was in the seventeenth
century that the Dutch, English and French East India Companies first
imported printed silks and cottons from the Far East. By that time crudely
block-printed textiles were being printed in the West, but they could not be
washed, as the colour only lay on the surface. The imported cloths, however,
were colourfast, as the Indians had perfected the technique of mordant

IKEA's lively contemporary fabrics prove that
modern prints take their inspiration from anywhere
and everywhere. They can be uninhibited in terms
of colour and motif, varying from the naïve to the
sophisticated, from the subtle to the brash.

dyeing—fixing the dye with a mordant (metal salt) such as alum or iron. The imported cloths, which were often hand-painted as well as printed, were a huge success. By the end of the seventeenth century, a number of printworks had been set up to produce imitation Indian cloths. But because of a series of English and French "anti-cloth" laws designed to protect the home-based woollen and silk industries, block printing developed slowly during the first half of the eighteenth century.

As in India, the cloth was printed by hand using wood blocks, one for each colour, carved with a reverse image raised in relief. The early blocks, which were about 30 × 20 cm/12 × 8 inches in size, were made entirely from wood. Because it was impossible to carve intricate detail in the wood, however, copper and brass pieces were being inserted into the wood for fine detail by the 1770s. An elaborate block took months to carve, but in the 1840s stereotyping was introduced for small repeat patterns. With this, pewter or zinc plates were cast from a single wooden mould of a pattern repeat, then fitted on to the face of the block, thus speeding up the process of block making considerably.

In printing, the cloth was gummed or pinned on to a printing table, which could be as much as 17 metres/19 yards long. The block would be charged with mordant or dye, then stamped on to the cloth, using a mallet to ensure a good impression. The process was repeated along the length of cloth. A second colour would not be printed until the first had dried. Exact placement of the blocks was essential for accurate colour registration, so pins at the corners of each block were used.

Block printing was painstaking, and a good block printer could cover only

ABOVE LEFT: Jacobean crewelwork has often provided inspiration for textiles destined for "Tudorbethan" homes, as in "Huntingdon", a printed linen produced by Liberty in the 1950s.

ABOVE CENTRE: This screen printed cotton, also produced by Liberty, is called "Bauhaus" and takes its inspiration from a tapestry woven at the influential German Bauhaus school of design (1919–1933), which advocated Modernism and influenced many designers and architects. The print was designed by Susan Collier in 1971.

ABOVE RIGHT: This
block-printed cotton had
a very different source of
inspiration: the sight of
thrushes creeping under
the fruit nets at William
Morris's country home in
Oxfordshire. Entitled
"The Strawberry Thief",
it was designed by
Morris in 1883.

about 30 metres/ 33 yards of fabric a day. But the technique produced bright,
varied colour with a unique softness and depth of colour created by allowing
each colour to dry before printing further colours. Although the industry
was at its height in the late eighteenth century, it was still the most common
fabric printing process in the early nineteenth century. After that, however,
block printing was gradually overtaken by roller printing (see page 68).
Often the two methods were combined, with block printing being used to
finish a roller-printed cloth. In Victorian times block printing was used for
high-quality furnishing fabrics and for paisley shawls imitating the original
woven designs. It was also used by William Morris (using natural dyes) and
the Arts and Crafts movement. Both modern and traditional patterns were
blocked-printed in the 1920s and '30s, but by the 1960s block printing was no
longer commercially viable, and most companies who had used the process
for producing document fabrics (faithful reproductions of designs from the
past) were forced to abandon it.

⌒ Copperplate-printed Toiles ⌒

At the same time as block printing was at its zenith, the technique of printing
from a flat copper plate was well established, appearing first in Ireland in
1752 and by the early 1760s flourishing in several London printworks.
Between 1760 and 1800 furnishing fabrics produced by this method were
very fashionable. Printed in single colours such as red, blue, blackish-brown
or purple on undyed calico, they were finely detailed, delicate and sophisticated. Latterly, the best-known of the copperplate-printed fabrics were the
scenic designs known as "toiles", after the *toiles de Jouy* (see page 174) printed

LEFT: Though the *toiles de Jouy* of France were latterly the most famous of this type of monochrome copperplate print, several printworks in Ireland and England specialized in similar finely detailed copperplate prints. This linen-and-cotton "toile" shows scenes from David Garrick's "Lethe, or Aesop in the Shades" and was produced in England c. 1766–1774.

from the 1770s by the Oberkampf factory at Jouy, near Versailles. The method was employed for printing on silk too, but inks were generally used for this rather than dyes.

For copperplate printing, the design was engraved in reverse on to a flat copper plate. The mordant was applied to the plate then wiped off, leaving colour only below the smooth surface of the plate. This was transferred to the cloth by pressing the fabric and plate together in a printing press. The process allowed variations of shading because it was relatively easy to cut fine lines. Subtle variations in depth of tone could be achieved by altering the spacing and width of the lines; the darkest areas were made by cross-hatching.

The affinity of this method with paper engravings (which employed virtually the same process except that printer's ink was used instead of mordant) meant that engravings were a popular source of design.

⌒ The Export Market in Fabrics ⌒

During the late eighteenth century Britain founded an export industry which stretched round the globe. It was the principal supplier of textiles to America, which took more than half of Britain's cotton exports and also a high proportion of its wool.

France's "anti-cloth" laws, which banned the importation and imitation of Indian calicoes in order to protect the Lyon silk weavers (see page 26), discouraged the development of the cotton weaving and printing industry until 1759, when the bans were removed. The Alsatian city of Mulhouse, which was a free imperial city until it was annexed by France at the end of the

RIGHT: The Alsatian city of Mulhouse became a centre for cotton spinning, weaving and printing in the eighteenth century. This design from a French textile printer's pattern book, probably from Mulhouse, c. 1795–1800, is typical of the floral prints (imitating Indian calicoes) which were produced in the region.

eighteenth century, had several thriving printworks (the first established in 1746) and became the centre for the new, largely Protestant-based industry that spread throughout the upper Rhine area, bringing with it spinning and weaving enterprises. During the nineteenth century training schools were set up, technical commissions organized and a documentation centre for designers created, which is today The Museum of Printed Textiles. The Haussmann Company from nearby Colmar was one of the most important manufacturing companies outside Mulhouse, producing printed cottons, woolstuffs, linens and silks of the highest quality that were exported throughout Europe.

⌐ Roller-printed Cottons ⌐

From the beginning of the nineteenth century, roller printing was increasingly used by furnishing fabric manufacturers, as it was a less expensive method of producing small prints. A big advantage of rollers was that they could avoid breaks in line or overlaps, but their disadvantage was that repeats were limited to the circumference of the roller.

Most rollers had an engraved copper surface and, like flat copper plates, produced very fine detail. Machines with wooden rollers, however, could cope better with flat areas of colour. "Mule", or "union", machines, which combined copper and wooden rollers, offered the best of both worlds, producing quite complex patterns. Many roller-printed textiles were also finished with hand block printing.

As with copperplate-printed fabrics, engravings were an obvious first source of inspiration for designs, although these were superseded by floral patterns. In the late nineteenth century, Japanese motifs were very fashionable and their small scale made them eminently suitable. The quality of roller prints depended to a large extent on the skill of the cylinder maker. Engraving was traditionally done with a sharp tool, though the technique of stippling, which was very popular from the mid-1840s to the mid-1860s, involved hammering with a blunt point. Rollers were produced by specialist engravers and were sold to printers at home and abroad. England exported many to the United States for use in its developing roller-printing industry. The leading English engraver and cylinder maker of the first half of the nineteenth century was Joseph Lockett of Manchester (where the English roller-printing industry was concentrated).

The technique of rainbow printing, which had originally been developed in the mid 1820s by block printers, was adapted in the 1830s to roller printing. With this, subtly shaded tones could be created by printing stripes of colour that would blend together on contact.

Roller printing is still in limited use today, mainly for long runs of inexpensive cottons. A modern machine, which is based on one originally

OVERLEAF: The designs for these fresh and pretty cotton prints were based on patterns found on Victorian pottery, which may in turn have been inspired by motifs on Oriental ceramics and textiles. The coordinating fabrics and pottery are the brainchild of Putnam's, a London antique shop which exports them all over the world.

devised in 1783, consists of a large rotating central cylinder over which a thick endless blanket passes. The blanket, covered with a backing fabric, supports the cloth as it passes through the machine. The design is engraved on printing rollers, one per colour, each of which has a rotating roller supplying the colour paste, and blades to remove excess paste and lint. As many as sixteen rollers may be used to print one design, though the process is more often used for designs incorporating just one or two colours.

The modern process of engraving a roller is a far cry from Joseph Lockett's day. Today the design is often transferred to the roller by computer graphics; after the areas not to be printed are coated with a chemical-resistant paint, the roller is dipped in acid to etch the design, and finally the resin coat is removed and the roller polished.

⌒ Screen-printed Textiles ⌒

Early in the twentieth century, hand silk-screen printing of fabric was developed, and is still in use today. Based on the same principle as stencilling, it is done on a frame over which a screen of silk muslin is stretched. There is

one screen for each colour of the design. The design is transferred to the screen, and the areas that are not to print are masked out with wax, card or paper. Colour paste is then pushed through the unmasked parts of the screen on to the cloth underneath. Hand screen printing was developed commercially in France, Britain and the United States in the 1930s and it was during the 1950s that it really came into its own. Screens could duplicate almost all the styles of other printing techniques. They were cheaper to make and easier to experiment with and to change.

By the 1960s commercial screen printing was mechanized. At a time when patterned weaves were very expensive, semi-automatic or fully automatic flat-bed screen printing made it possible to produce reasonably priced fabrics. Today, most screens are metal cylinders and have been engraved photographically. The vast majority of printed textiles are produced using these rotary screen printers.

Screen printing led to designs with a very specific look, more like block prints than roller prints, with an angular, sketch-like, energetic quality.

⟶ Other Fabric-printing Processes ⟵

Heat-transfer printing, another twentieth-century process, involves printing the design on paper with special dyes, then transferring the pattern on to the cloth by passing the fabric through a hot calender. It is possible to transfer large photographs, pictorial prints and imitation figured-weave effects.

Photographic printing employs a photographic process to print a design on fabric. The cloth is first treated with a light-reactive chemical, then a negative is placed on the fabric, light is transmitted to it and the colour is developed. After it stabilizes, the fabric is washed and the print becomes permanent.

Resist printing is an age-old process used all around the world. The cloth is first printed with a resist such as resin, fat, starch or wax, which prevents these areas from accepting colour when dyed; after printing, the resist is removed. Batik, which utilizes hot wax as a resist, is the oldest method of resist printing. Modern commercial forms of resist printing follow a similar principle, applying a resist that prevents the colour from fixing.

Discharge printing involves dyeing the fabric first with a background colour, then treating the pattern area with a reducing agent contained in a print paste, which removes the dye from the treated areas. Either the discharged area is left white, or it is coloured by a dye which is contained in the print paste and not affected by the reducing agent.

⟶ Early Paper Hangings ⟵

Like textiles, the first wallpapers—or paper hangings, as they were called—were hand printed using woodblocks. Not much is known about the earliest

"Stones of Bath", a Sanderson's screen-printed cotton designed by artist John Piper in 1962.

paper hangings, for, until recently, there had been little research into wallpaper. Much sixteenth- and seventeenth-century wallpaper still lies hidden beneath layers of paper, paint or panelling. Paper is obviously much more fragile than fabric and so less likely to survive the ravages of time, but it has also often tended to be regarded as the poor relation of fabric. Recently, however, there has been a recognition that wallpaper is of interest in its own right, and serious research is now being carried out into its history. This has been made easier by several interesting finds, notably at Temple Newsam, a sixteenth-century country house in the north of England, where, during redecoration, fragments of about a hundred eighteenth- and nineteenth-century wallpapers were found. Some of them have been reproduced by Zoffany and, indeed, are again adorning the walls of the house. The British National Trust also owns houses where original wallpapers can be seen in their appropriate settings, and in the United States, "document" (historic)

wallpapers can be seen in reconstructed historic villages such as Williamsburg, Virginia and Shelburne, Vermont. There are also a number of museums with interesting collections, in both the United States and Britain.

The earliest known use of wallpaper was in China in AD 206, where drawn or printed designs related to funeral rites were used on the walls of houses and temples. In Europe its first known use was in the fifteenth century, and it does not appear to have been in general use elsewhere before then. Decorations for walls at this time included patterns stencilled on to plaster; decorative paper hangings provided a practical alternative to these. Tapestries were also a popular form of wall decoration, and wallpaper made a relatively inexpensive substitute.

The earliest surviving fragment of English wallpaper was found at Christ's College, Cambridge; it had been block printed on the back of a set of documents from 1509 and was patterned with a pine cone or pomegranate design in imitation of the Italian velvets or damasks which were very much in fashion then. (The process of printing rough designs imitating textiles was known at the time as "damasking", and it was standard practice to do this on waste paper such as old proof copies or condemned literature.)

Early paper hangings were block printed in black (or sometimes dark blue or red) ink by craftsmen known as paper-stainers. The sheets measured about 30 × 36 cm/12 × 15 inches, which was the size that would fit into the flat sieves used to drain the shredded cloth during paper manufacture. Most of these early wallpapers have been found, not on walls, but lining coffers, deed boxes, chests and cupboards or serving as endpapers in books. They were different, however, from the binding papers and lining papers that were also used for these purposes, since the wallpapers were printed with designs not complete in themselves; they were meant to be assembled into an overall design on walls.

Sixteenth- and seventeenth-century designs included the Tudor rose, coats of arms and other heraldic motifs, as well as outdoor scenes, flowers, fruit, masks, strapwork and imitations of black-stitch embroidery. Some of these papers may have been used as borders, above wainscoting. Although uncoloured papers were preferred during the seventeenth century, coloured papers were nevertheless in use. Often the papers were brushed with a watercolour ground prior to block printing. Stencilled colour was also sometimes used in combination with block printing, but the block-printed outlines rarely corresponded precisely to the stencilled areas, and it was difficult to prevent the colour from smudging.

By the end of the seventeenth century wallpapers were in general use by the middle and lower classes but had not attracted the interest of the wealthy. Fragments of papers found in great houses suggest that wallpapers were first used in the servants' quarters of these homes. They became acceptable in the

Chinese wallpapers were prized in the eighteenth century, particularly for bedrooms. European imitations were also produced, but genuine Chinese papers, such as this one from the King's Rooms, Belvoir Castle, were more true to life.

great houses only when they successfully imitated luxurious fabrics and other expensive materials. With this in mind, London's Blew Paper Warehouse in 1702 advertised "the true sorts of Figured Paper Hangings . . . in the manner of real Tapistry, and in imitation of Irish stitch, and flowered Damask and also of marble and other Coloured Wainscot, fitt for the hanging of rooms . . ."

∽ Up-market Papers of the Eighteenth Century ∽

Wallpaper took a giant step up the social scale at the end of the seventeenth century with the development of English flock papers in imitation of Italian velvets. The process of flocking had been used in England for at least two hundred years, and flocked papers were manufactured in the seventeenth century, but they didn't actually become fashionable until the early eighteenth century. When the architect William Kent replaced textile hangings in the King's Great Drawing Room at Kensington Palace with the "new-fangled flock paper", he set a fashion that was to last until the present day. At around this time, the Whitehall offices of the Privy Council were decorated with a crimson flock paper that became fashionable for grand rooms of the neo-Palladian houses of the period. Flocks enjoyed the greatest popularity between about 1715 and 1745. They were fashionable in their own right, but the price worked in their favour, too: whereas a cut velvet of the 1740s cost 25 shillings a yard, a flock paper was only around 4 shillings a yard.

The process involved applying a slow-drying adhesive or varnish to a painted ground using a leather and oilcloth stencil or a woodblock, then sprinkling powdered wool (left over from the manufacture of cloth) on to the wet design, to form a raised pattern resembling velvet pile. Colours were largely limited to one shade for the ground and a second for the flocking. Later in the century, smaller patterns and multi-coloured wools were introduced. In subsequent centuries powdered pigments, cotton, silk and nylon were tried as alternatives to wool, and today synthetic fibres are blown with a spray gun on to the paper. Otherwise the technique remains much the same, and flock papers in traditional eighteenth-century designs are still made by a number of manufacturers.

Flock paper was hung in the most important rooms of a house, but another popular wallpaper of the time, the so-called China or India paper (see page 186), was favoured for bedrooms. These hand-painted papers, which were the height of fashion from about 1740 to 1790, were imported from China by the East India Company. They were beyond the means of most people, but a wider market was soon catered for, and imitations of the papers were being produced in England and on the Continent. Initially these Chinese-style papers, like other papers produced at the time, were hand-drawn and hand-coloured, or the outlines were block-printed (or sometimes etched) and the colours added by hand or by stencil. Later, as printing techniques improved, the colours themselves were block printed (though colouring by hand did not disappear until the end of the century).

Much of the pioneering work in multi-coloured block printing was done by John Baptist Jackson, a leading English paper-stainer of the day and one of the few whose work has survived. Jackson used only oil colours, which were subsequently overtaken by distemper. Nevertheless, his wallpapers, which he designed and manufactured himself, revolutionized the wall decoration of his time and remained popular until the end of the century. Jackson was influenced by the work of the Italian Renaissance chiaroscuro engravers, and his chiaroscuro printing technique involved printing from two or more monochrome blocks to produce a three-dimensional effect of light and shade. He described his work as follows:

> By this way of printing Paper, the Inventor has contrived that the lights and Shades shall be broad and bold, and give great relief to the Figures;

John Baptist Jackson, a leading English "paper-stainer" of the eighteenth century, pioneered the technique of printing wallpapers using monochrome blocks. Jackson specialized in styles of the Old Masters. This paper by Jackson is based on landscapes by the artist Marco Ricci.

the finest prints of all the antique Statues which imitate Drawings are
introduced into Niches of Chiaro Oscuro in the Pannels of their Paper;
these are surrounded with a Mosaic Work, in Imitation of Frames,
or with Festoons and Garlands of Flowers, with great Elegance
and Taste.

The Block Printing and Hanging of Papers

By the end of the eighteenth century, sheets of paper measuring about 54 cm/
$22\frac{1}{2}$ inches × 77-84 cm/32-35 inches were being pasted together, a dozen at a
time, into a strip about 10.5 metres/$11\frac{1}{2}$ yards long. The dimensions of a roll
of wallpaper today are based on this. The strip of paper, which was made
from high-quality rag, was first painted with a ground colour then printed in

several colours with carved pearwood blocks, using one block per colour. Each colour was allowed to dry before the next was printed, which created a depth of colour that is not possible in modern "wet on wet" printing. The effect was enhanced by the tendency of the thick distemper to stand slightly proud of the surface, which was due to the suction created when the block was lifted off the paper.

For patterns requiring fine detail, brass wires and pins were hammered into the printing surface of the wood block. The early "pin prints", with minute dots between the main motifs, were produced in this way.

There were various ways actually to hang paper. Early methods included simply nailing, tacking or pasting the paper on to the plaster. Alternatively, the paper was pasted on to a backing of scrim or canvas then tacked on to battens fastened to the walls, in the same way as textiles were hung. Nails or tacks were hidden by braid or by a decorative fillet (made from carved and gilded wood, cast lead, papier mâché, or cord dipped in gesso and then painted or gilded). Alternatively, paper borders might be used.

⟶ International Influences ⟵

Britain did not import many wallpapers from the Continent during the eighteenth century, but British "stained papers" were exported in large

"Blue paper" was a name given to wallpaper in the eighteenth century, when indigo was the only dye exempt from taxes. Sometimes, as in this early eighteenth century hand-blocked and stencilled example, shades of brown were added.

quantities all over the world. In Europe, especially in Italy, they were used not only as wall hangings but also as covers and endpapers of books and linings for cupboards and drawers. The fashion for flock wallpapers, in particular, spread to France, where society ladies eagerly replaced their Gobelins tapestries with the English "blue papers". ("Blue papers" was another name for wallpapers, stemming from the vogue for coordinating paper and fabric. At that time, only blue patterned linen was available, due to the indigo dyers' exemption from legislation—designed to protect the flax and woollen industries—prohibiting the use of printed, painted, stained or dyed calicoes. Hence the preponderance of blue papers, to coordinate with the blue fabrics.) Towards the end of the eighteenth century, however, political upheaval on the Continent led to a reduction in demand for British papers in Europe.

Large volumes of papers had also been exported to America (which had no wallpaper factories of its own until 1765, when the first opened in New York). In fact, it was the custom for an eighteenth-century American bridegroom to present his new wife with a set of English paper hangings. But after the War of Independence, American papers came increasingly from France. There was a huge U.S. demand for the nineteenth-century French scenic papers (see page 188) in particular, and some American homes today still contain sets of these now-exclusive papers.

The scenic papers were the culmination of an intense effort by the French to develop their wallpaper industry. In a very short time they had perfected block-printing techniques learned from the British and were producing vast quantities of high-quality papers. France's leading eighteenth-century paper-stainer was Jean Baptiste Réveillon. His Neoclassical, Pompeian-style papers are among the most artistic wallpapers ever produced and were intended to give ordinary people the opportunity to have grand interiors too. (Ironically, Réveillon's factory was the first to be attacked and destroyed during the French Revolution, and he retired to England.) The earliest French scenic papers were produced towards the end of the eighteenth century, but these were hand-painted; the printed papers did not appear until the nineteenth century. Using assemblies of blocks which might be several metres/yards in length, some of the scenic papers were 16 metres/17 yards long and 3 metres/13 feet high. They formed a continuous picture around the four walls of a room, without a single repeat.

By contrast with the French government, which provided incentives to improve the standard of design, the British government continued to levy burdensome taxes and licence fees on its paper-stainers. But when French papers, by now the best in Europe, started coming into England in the early nineteenth century, their popularity and quality galvanized the British into competitive action. The wallpaper taxes and licence fees were finally removed, and the prohibition against using the cheaper straw and woodpulp instead of rag in the manufacture of paper was lifted.

⟶ The Age of Mass Production ⟶

These new developments in the wallpaper manufacturing industry coincided with the arrival of power-driven machinery. Early in the nineteenth century, a machine capable of producing "continuous" paper was developed (though in Britain its use was not permitted by the Excise until 1830); this paper was thinner than the earlier paper, which was more like card. Shortly after, a machine that could print from curved stereotyped plates on continuous paper was invented. Experiments with roller-printing machines already used for printing cotton (see page 68) finally bore fruit, and wallpapers were printed by these machines from the late 1830s. Embossed, twilled and gilded papers, and satin papers, which were rubbed with French chalk to add a sheen, were other achievements of the time. The first synthetic dyes (see page 56) appeared around the middle of the century. (At first their arsenical formulations were a health hazard, as several people were taken ill when they breathed in particles, and some children died through licking green paper hangings. But by the 1870s manufacturers were advertising their papers as "arsenic-free".) Technical progress in wallpaper manufacture continued throughout the nineteenth century, though the standard of design and workmanship declined. The age of mass production was underway.

Soon virtually every house boasted papered walls. Not only were wallpapers within the means of ordinary people, but they were cheap enough to

Sprig wallpapers were popular in the eighteenth and early nineteenth centuries. The original wallpaper bearing the English interior design firm Colefax & Fowler's "Berkeley Sprig" pattern (shown here on cloth) was discovered by the firm's co-founder John Fowler, underneath a silk damask wallcovering in the Grand Saloon at Berkeley Square, London. It is thought to have been inspired by a late seventeenth- or early eighteenth-century embroidered quilt.

replace within four or five years. Previously their expense had made them relatively permanent parts of a house. (A green flock at Temple Newsam, for example, was removed after 81 years, to be replaced with a red flock—which survived for 113 years.)

"Sprig" papers were already popular and, in the early nineteenth century, floral designs and small geometric patterns also became fashionable. Many were on a pin dot ground, a style that had been adapted to cylinder printing machines from the original wood block printing technique (see page 78). At about this time it became standard practice to regard particular papers as more suitable for certain rooms. Bedrooms were hung with floral or chintz patterns or moiré patterns, which imitated watered silk. Marble paper was often used for halls and staircases, and flocks were still fashionable for drawing rooms, dining rooms and libraries.

Sprigs and moiré patterns were still popular by the 1840s, along with trellis designs, patterns imitating swagged textiles or painted panelling, and Neoclassical borders that looked like architectural mouldings. The popularity of the Gothic Revival style resulted in a large number of complicated Gothic designs and geometric patterns. The architect A W N Pugin was the best-known of the Gothic Revival designers; it was he who designed the paper and decoration for London's new Houses of Parliament in 1847.

⌐ Higher Standards of Design ⌐

Pugin's "Medieval Court" proved to be the most popular exhibit at the Great Exhibition of 1851. This showcase of Victorian goods, which actually served

The architect and designer Owen Jones was active in the reform movements which attempted to raise design standards in the second half of the nineteenth century. His own work was highly structured and formalized, as in this wallpaper designed by Jones c. 1852–1874 for the Viceroy of Cairo and hand block-printed by Jeffrey & Company.

to highlight the low standard of mass-market design prevalent at the time, triggered off the design reform movements of the second half of the century (see page 44). The writings of Owen Jones, John Ruskin and Charles Eastlake were all influential, and the designs of William Morris and the Arts and Crafts movement (see pages 46 and 157) had an enormous impact. Morris, who advocated traditional skills and craftsmanship, revived the technique of wood block printing using vegetable dyes. He began a new era in wallpaper production, raising the whole level of design. Ironically, it was the work of Morris—who actually regarded wallpapers as mere substitutes

ABOVE: This "Bird and Flower" paper, produced by Jeffrey & Company c. 1880, was designed specifically for dados. Related frieze and filling papers were also produced.

ABOVE: Washable "sanatory" wallpapers were a late-Victorian development. Like this one, designed in 1895, they tended to have a brownish finish, caused by the varnish.

for tapestries or hangings of embroidery or chintz—which led to wallpaper for the first time being treated as a respectable medium in its own right.

To help lift the general standard of wallpaper design, Jeffrey & Company, the firm that had taken over the production of Morris's designs, began commissioning artists and architects, including Owen Jones, Walter Crane, William Burges, E W Godwin and Charles Eastlake, to design wallpapers for them. One type of paper they designed, introduced by the company in the 1870s, consisted of three patterns—for the frieze, filling and dado—in one overall design. Angled versions were even available for stairwells.

⌐ New Directions in Wallpaper ⌐

Among the most prolific of the Jeffrey & Company artists was Walter Crane, a well-known illustrator of children's books whose work was also very influential in textile designs of the time. Crane was the first artist to create papers specifically for the nursery. His earliest nursery paper was produced in 1875. One of his most charming was "Briar Rose", featuring Sleeping Beauty, the Prince, the sleeping servants, peacocks and the rose itself rambling over the entire paper. Other illustrators who designed nursery papers included Kate Greenaway, Randolph Caldecott, Mabel L Attwell, Cecil Aldin, John Hassall and Will Owen.

The Aesthetic movement (see pages 44 and 156) produced a number of wallpaper designs at the end of the nineteenth century; Bruce J Talbert and E W Godwin were the principal Aesthetic designers. Art Nouveau (see page 129) also influenced wallpapers, with C F A Voysey, George Walton and Harry Napper the leading British exponents of this style.

Art Nouveau designs predominated too in the new patterned friezes introduced in the late nineteenth century. By this time it had become fashionable to remove dados from walls, and fill the area from picture rail to skirting with a plain printed or textured wallcovering. As a result, patterned wallpaper friezes became extremely popular, particularly those of William Shand Kydd. His friezes were hand-blocked and stencilled, a technique that had not been used since the seventeenth century. Several years after setting up his firm, Shand Kydd employed five block printers and a dozen or so stencillers; he often delivered rolls to customers himself in a hired barrow that he wheeled along London's Oxford Street. Shand Kydd Ltd subsequently became one of the largest wallpaper manufacturers of the time. (By the 1920s, however, patterned friezes were being replaced by cut-out decorations with clumps of hanging foliage, combined with textured fillings.)

Other late Victorian developments in wallpaper included the development of "sanatories" (see page 136)—the first truly washable papers, which were printed in transparent oils or varnish colours, and which remained popular well into the twentieth century—and the increased popularity of raised or

embossed papers, marketed by such firms as Lincrusta Walton and Ana-glypta. By the end of the nineteenth century, more than forty large firms were producing wallpaper in Britain. In 1899 some of the largest firms formed the Wallpaper Manufacturers Ltd, in order to provide financial support for smaller member firms still using hand-printing methods.

⌒ U.S. Wallpaper Production in the Nineteenth Century ⌒

At the beginning of the nineteenth century there were only a handful of wallpaper printers in the United States, but by the end of the century there were fifty. Philadelphia, Boston and New York were the chief manufacturing centres. The Philadelphia firm Howell and Brothers became the largest wallpaper manufacturer of the 1860s and '70s, having imported the first wallpaper printing machine in 1844. As in Europe, mass production methods led to the rapid expansion of the industry during this period.

Like Jeffrey & Company in England, the New York firm Warren Fuller & Company commissioned leading designers, such as Louis C Tiffany, Candace Wheeler and Lockwood de Forest, to create wallpapers. Tiffany's work has been described as "the last expression of the American Gothic", and, in fact, the popularity of the American Gothic style (see page 41) created an enormous public demand for complicated and ornate papers.

⌒ Nineteenth-century Continental Papers ⌒

Elaborate designs proliferated in France, too, in the nineteenth century, particularly those imitating tapestries, Eastern silks and Italian velvets. By the middle of the century, there were three hundred wallpaper factories in Paris alone. But it was not until the Art Deco style emerged after the First World War that French wallpaper design took a fresh new direction.

Wallpaper was not so popular in Germany at the beginning of the nineteenth century as in England or France, though there were a number of wallpaper printers throughout Germany. In the first half of the century, Germans invented the *irisé* effect (a grounding in which delicately blended colours merge) and also "Perlmutt" (mother-of-pearl effect) wallpapers.

⌒ Twentieth-century Papers ⌒

During the First World War, wallpaper production virtually ceased; indeed, some of the machines were adapted to producing shell bodies instead. After the War, the wide variety of patterns that had previously been available was mainly replaced by "Jazz Age" designs (see page 112) or plain papers with appliqué borders. Art Deco (see pages 113 and 137) and Oriental-style designs were also popular at around this time.

As regards technology, there were relatively few advances in the wallpaper industry during the first half of the twentieth century, but the 1950s and '60s

In nineteenth-century France, as in England, papers that imitated expensive textiles were still particularly popular. The rich orange, red and black of this French flock wallpaper of the period help to enhance the appearance of velvet provided by the flock.

brought more developments in manufacture than any previous period. The improvement of plastic coatings increased durability and simplified maintenance of wallpapers. Screen-printing was adapted to wallpaper manufacture in the early 1950s and encouraged the use of patterns with lively, contemporary motifs; high-speed techniques were soon developed. In the 1960s photogravure was increasingly used, at first, particularly, for dramatic, large-scale modern designs. Today, wallpaper is primarily manufactured by rotary screen printing, rotogravure, flexography and ink-embossing techniques.

Yet despite, or perhaps because of, the increasing sophistication of the technology available for wallpaper manufacture, the late twentieth century has seen a phenomenal growth of interest in document wallpapers, which emerged from the "English country-house" look, developed by the decorator John Fowler in particular. Traditional designs and chintz patterns characterize the wallpapers used for this look, as well as the small-scale patterns which were fashionable early in the nineteenth century and which become popular again in the 1970s. Although modern screen printing methods are used for the majority of the historic papers reproduced today, a small number are still hand blocked (by Cole & Son and Sanderson) using the original wood blocks and virtually the same techniques.

CHAPTER FOUR

ABSTRACT PATTERN

"All ornament should be based on
a geometrical construction."
OWEN JONES, *The Grammar of Ornament*, 1856

Abstract design, like abstract art, can be classified as either semi-abstract (in which the motifs are based on nature or known objects, though they bear little resemblance to natural forms) or pure abstract (in which the shapes and colours are of the artist's own invention).

Abstract patterns used in wallpapers and fabrics today are not easy to trace back to any particular source. One pattern may take its inspiration from a variety of places and times and add a contemporary aspect to it. In the early days, patterns usually had religious significance or had to do with the status of those who would use them. In the twentieth century they may have more to do with an admiration of science or technology than with religion. Many different cultures use similar or identical patterns, perhaps because of the limitations of materials or techniques, or because designs have been passed on from one part of the world to another. The source of much inspiration is images seen while travelling.

The Welsh architect and designer Owen Jones in 1856 published *The Grammar of Ornament*, in which he illustrated architectural decoration he had seen on his tours of the Middle East and Spain, as well as "ornament of savage tribes" from the South Pacific. The book set out the principles of good design, particularly in the use of colour, and Jones hoped to encourage designers to understand the underlying principles behind the art of different cultures. He did not want designers to copy the patterns slavishly but to use them as inspiration in creating new, rational, formalized patterns. Jones

A page illustrating Celtic ornament, from *The Grammar
of Ornament*, Owen Jones's great chromo-lithographed tome.
Published in 1856, it has been highly inspirational
for architects and designers ever since.

decreed that "all ornament should be based on a geometrical construction" and that realistic "flowers or other natural objects should not be used as ornaments". In his own work, nature was conventionalized to an almost mathematical degree, with highly structured repeats; his floral motifs were reduced to formalized symmetrical shapes, and colour relationships were based on mathematical proportions. *The Grammar of Ornament*, which has recently been reprinted, was enormously influential and has been used as a sourcebook by designers of weaves and prints alike, ever since its publication. Jones's example also encouraged other architects to become involved in industrial design.

⏤ Egyptian Motifs ⏤

Only a very few examples of actual Egyptian fabrics exist from earlier than the fourteenth century BC. Linen fabrics with semi-abstract designs in red, blue and green linen thread depicting birds and lotus flowers were found in an Eighteenth Dynasty tomb, c. 1450 BC. However, representations of very early hangings have been found in the wall paintings of some tombs. Those found in a Third Dynasty tomb, c. 2650 BC, were patterned with stars and chevrons in blue, brown and amber. There are also representations of early Egyptian patterned fabrics in wall paintings of a Twelfth Dynasty rock-cut tomb at Beni Hasan, c. 1950 BC. These include a star pattern from the dress of Hotept, wife of Amenemhet, and chevrons and frets from the clothing of their son Chnemhotep.

There was a great variety of these very early abstract woven patterns. Some were based on the lotus and papyrus, symbolizing food for the body and mind. The feathers of exotic birds were represented, and so were the palm branch and the twisted cords of palm stems. Fish or snake scales, diamond patterns, rows of aster heads, key or fret patterns, fylfots (swastika-like emblems), zigzags, scrolls and numerous geometric inventions were used, all in considerable variety but with great discipline. The colours were rusty browns, grey-greens, blues and yellows with black and white. There are a number of designs consisting of pyramid and diamond shapes in red superimposed on a white ground of cotton, linen, silk or mixtures of these.

When Egypt became part of the Islamic empire in the seventh century AD, many of the Egyptian patterns were taken up by the Arabs, who used them with a deeper turquoise and more florid shapes. The Greeks had used similar forms, but theirs were more curved and flexible, with wavy flower stems and breaking-wave patterns.

In the twentieth century, many Art Deco designers (see page 113) were inspired by the Egyptian forms and colours and by the Greek ones which followed them. In the 1920s in Paris, Sonia Delauney (see page 111) used Egyptian-like diamonds and stripes in bright and uninhibited colours for her exquisite fabrics. Modern hangings by such designers as Mary Spyrou have been inspired by the wall tiles of the Coptic people of Egypt. In the 1950s Swedish cotton screen-prints in uninhibited colours featured broken elongated diamond shapes or broken stripes also influenced by Egyptian

RIGHT: A number of twentieth-century designers have been influenced by Egyptian woven patterns such as in this integral tapestry woven band, which features angular volute motifs in delicate, thin lines on a rusty-red ground. The abstract character of the pattern suggests it was made in the three centuries after the Arab conquest of Egypt in 641.

OVERLEAF: The Gothic style was drawn from ecclesiastical decoration of the Middle Ages, though the "Gothick" style of the eighteenth century was more lighthearted and eclectic than the Victorian Gothic Revival a century later. Heavy velvets, brocades and damasks in rich colours typified the latter style.

patterns. "Karnak", designed for Warners by Jenny Lowndes in 1967, was a screen-printed cotton, part of the "Pharaoh" range and based on capital ornament from Egyptian columns.

⌒ Moorish Influences ⌒

From the fourteenth century, Spain—which had been ruled by the Moors since the eighth century—produced Islamic-inspired patterns such as stars, small pyramid shapes strung in rows, intricate lattices and rows of small motifs, often inside ogee frames. The Spanish patterning was dominated by geometric figures and arabesques, often in the "laceria" design which resembles interlaced canework. Intricate and very elegant Arabian inscriptions also appeared.

In the eighteenth century the Moroccans were weaving similar designs with wide bands of trellis, small propeller-like patterns in rows, stars and stylized rosettes. They appliquéd wool flannel tent squares with circles decorated with rays, stars, petals and zigzags.

In England, Moorish designs have lent themselves to flock wallpapers and luxurious velvets and silks in many periods, their rich exotic colours and shapes suiting the plush quality of the paper or fabric. In the late nineteenth century, Near Eastern textiles such as "Ottoman" velvets (which featured patterns based on ogees and pomegranates), kilims, shawls and embroideries were all the rage. They were often used in "Turkish corners" furnished with window seats, cushions and draperies.

∽ Celtic Motifs ∽

The Celts dominated much of central and western Europe, including the British Isles, from about 650 BC until the Roman conquest. Skilled metal workers, they excelled in stone carving and bronze and gold work. After the break-up of the Roman Empire in the fifth century, the Celts were the first of the barbaric peoples to produce a relatively sophisticated art based on that of the ancients, in particular Greece, Italy and the East. The influence of Celtic art spread right across Europe and for centuries inspired the decorative arts, including, later, fabric and wallpaper design.

The style is characterized by intricate yet very disciplined linear patterns. For example, two or three spiral lines starting at one point twist together into convoluted runic knots. Animals, birds and lizards may be elongated almost beyond recognition and intertwined in sinuous shapes which are sometimes symmetrical but often irregular. Compasswork, too, was typical of Celtic designs. The exuberantly embellished letters of illuminated manuscripts such as the Book of Kells were another major aspect of Celtic art. Later illuminated manuscripts often have intricate knotted patterns which are very reminiscent of Celtic designs.

∽ Gothic Style ∽

The Gothic style, which prevailed in western Europe from the twelfth to the sixteenth centuries, began with architecture. Derived originally from Middle Eastern sources, it is epitomized by the great medieval cathedrals and churches of Europe, with their pointed arches, ribbed vaults, emphasis on vertical lines, and intricate window tracery. Gothic motifs have their origin in ecclesiastical decoration, which, towards the end of the Gothic period, became very rich and elaborate. They included in particular the trefoil and quatrefoil, the pointed arch and, later, the ogee. Gothic ornament sometimes used motifs similar to Classical ornament, such as the acanthus leaf and the rosette, but they were much more stylized. Compasswork, as in Gothic crosses ornamented with geometrical motifs, was also a feature; this may have been based on old Celtic compasswork designs.

From the early eighteenth century, many buildings were erected in what was believed to be the Gothic style, influencing decoration in general. In the

This lion, symbol of Mark the Evangelist, is from the mid-7th century "Book of Durrow" and is surrounded by typically Celtic intertwined shapes.

"Gothic", a woven silk fabric from Watts & Company, was one of the company's earliest designs and has been in continuous production since 1874. It was designed by one of the firm's founders, the architect Thomas Garner, to enhance the buildings he and his partners were designing or restoring.

1740s Horace Walpole with great single-mindedness decorated his house at Strawberry Hill, near London, entirely in the Gothic (or Gothick, as the eighteenth-century version is often known) style. It became the most influential Gothick house of its day. Among all sorts of artefacts inspired by Gothic cathedrals and churches, Walpole used a wallpaper copied from a staircase paper in Worcester Cathedral.

The more uncompromising Gothic Revival of the nineteenth century, which occurred only in Britain and America, was spearheaded by the English architect A W N Pugin, who developed a faith in Gothic as the only honest style. Pugin designed dozens of wallpapers, many for the London decorator J G Crace. These formal, stylized patterns were all highly Gothic and included trefoils, thistles and monograms surrounded by entwined leaves, for such varied clients as the Duke of Devonshire and the Houses of Parliament. Robert Jones, who collaborated with Crace on the decoration of

the Royal Pavilion in Brighton, designed several wallpapers and borders in the Gothic style.

Among the many shapes adapted from Gothic architecture were the pointed arch, the columnar and ribbed constructions of churches, perpendicular windows, fluted vaulting, and the geometric tracery from wood and stone carving. Block printing lent itself to the regular square and diamond patterns containing single motifs which were a feature of this style. Oak leaves, four-petalled flower heads perhaps enclosed in ogee shapes, fleurs de lys in all sorts of guises, Tudor roses, crowns, heraldic animals and other emblems, star patterns and trellises were all good Gothic motifs.

American Indian Patterns

North American Indian patterns, though limited in number, are repeated in a great many variations, each of which is characteristic of a particular group, tribe or individual. There is a remarkable consistency in general style between patterns from prehistory and those of today, and old patterns are often revived.

Horizontal stripes and borders appear commonly, as well as zigzags, chequered patterns, stepped motifs and volutes. (The volute is a spiral scroll inspired by a marine shell similar to the whelk; this very abstract pattern can have stepped edges.) Bead patterns were often pictographs recording treaties between Indians and the U.S. government. The Indians, like the Greeks, use key patterns divided into three, four, five or six segments, producing rich variations.

Many patterns used on Indian textiles are the result of other craft processes. For example, spirals and radiating patterns often rise naturally from basket coiling and wood carving, and feathered circles from shields.

The North American Indians traditionally use patterns which are not just decorations on everyday objects but which portray animals or fish whose spirits are thought to inhabit the natural world and have power to influence events. The images of these animals become the distinguishing symbol of a man, group or clan. The animal may have parts of its body separated and re-arranged to fill a particular space. In other designs the space may be entirely filled with separated animal elements often in the form of little faces. These designs are not random but follow strict rules.

Quill work is made with porcupine quills, softened in water, flattened and dyed, usually red, black, yellow and blue. Patterned panels are made and appliquéd to objects. The quills can be spliced by overlapping and different textures are created by folding or wrapping the quills over the thread in different ways.

Silk ribbon from France reached the northeastern part of America in the eighteenth century as part of the fur trade. Indian women used the ribbons to

This blanket woven by the American Navajo Indians features in red, black and white the diamond motif typical of "eye dazzler" patterns.

make appliquéd panels sewn on to garments of black, red or blue cloth. During the nineteenth and twentieth centuries, the Indians of the southern Great Lakes region have produced appliquéd ribbon panels bearing the European acorn and diamond shapes in mirrored patterns, stylized to such an extent they have become virtually abstract.

Some screen-printed silks produced by the Wiener Werkstätte (see page 133) in the 1920s were directly influenced by American Indian weaves, and in the 1940s Janet Anderson, too, was influenced by American Indian designs. In the 1990s, the Swedish designer Barbro Peterson's double weave "Arrow" in pinks, blues and yellows is a good example of inspiration without copying.

Probably the best known of the American Indian weavers are the Navajo, of Arizona and New Mexico. For several centuries they have used simple upright looms to weave distinctive and unique blankets and rugs. Coarse-textured and brilliantly coloured, they are made from wool, with deep blue or black, on a white ground, and very strong bands of colour broken by small rectangular areas. Their designs for lightweight blankets, saddle throws and bedding are probably based on the Mexican *serape*, a simple garment which uses black and white checks with diamond patterns in the middle. In some Navajo blankets the diamonds form the dominant feature; variations of this "eye dazzler" pattern are woven in different regions, but in all versions the diamonds are arranged so as to create the illusion of movement. In Navajo ponchos, shifts of alignment in the pattern are typical. The classic Navajo blanket consists of five stripes and nine blocks in natural colours of wool, with blue and red and some green and yellow. In the 1970s a number of American designers were inspired by the Navajo stripes, and, in particular, a strippable wallpaper called "Pueblo" by Winfield Design Associates Inc was featured in interior decorating books and magazines.

Originally the most common source for the coloured yarn used by the Navajo was the bright red *bayeta*, a lightweight woollen cloth which in this case had been dyed red with cochineal before being imported by the Spanish in Mexico for making up into military uniforms during their occupation of that country. The Navajos bought the cloth, took it to pieces and then re-spun the bright red fibres by hand.

⟶ Peruvian Motifs ⟵

Cotton-and-wool tapestries displaying some of the most skilled techniques ever used were woven by the early Peruvians on very simple looms. Used primarily as decorations for clothing, the tapestries featured strong colour contrasts and bold patterns.

The Incas were the last of the great South American cultures. From 1440 till 1530, when they were conquered by the Spanish, their empire expanded from a small area in Peru to a vast region stretching from Chile in the south to Ecuador in the north. Rules governed all aspects of everyday life, including what clothes were to be worn and by whom they should be woven. The most striking of their designs was a black and white chequerboard for tunics, the sides of which were sewn together with colourful striped bands.

However, the Peruvian tapestry weaving industry was established long before the Incas—as early as the sixth century. The techniques used by the early Peruvians were similar to those of the Egyptian Copts (see page 23). The cotton or wool weft-faced fabric had many separate wefts (one for each colour area of the design), completely covering the warp. A surprising number of tapestries from before the Spanish Conquest still exist, as they were preserved in graves. These show the Peruvian use of curvilinear wefts,

OVERLEAF: Kilims—flat, pileless rugs woven in the Near East, eastern Europe and India—are traditionally used as wall hangings, curtains or tent covers. Here, the wallpaper and borders are inspired by kilims, and the textiles are all traditional.

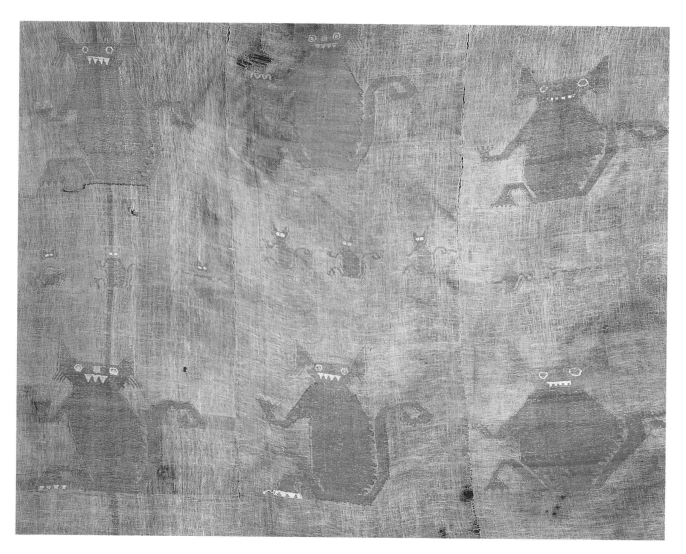

ABOVE: Peruvian weaving has a long and illustrious history. This portion of a pre-fifteenth century Peruvian shroud in cotton and vicuna is brocaded with coloured wools. The cats' tails form the volute motif often used in Peruvian weaving.

woven so skilfully that the "steps" that make up the curve are hardly to be seen and the cloth has no right or wrong side. Both geometrical and curvilinear designs are often outlined in black.

The range of colours used by the Peruvians has always been large, made up from just the three basic colours of blue, red and yellow. The blue dye came from indigo and produced shades from sky blue to midnight blue.

Early Peruvian motifs fall roughly into three groups. There are the stepped-volute (a spiral scroll with stepped edges) and a bisected eye with tear pendant, appearing in a diagonally divided rectangular field. There are the composite motifs combining several symbolic elements, including a symbol like the letter N. And there are the animals, birds and staff-bearing figures, which have become so abstracted as to be hardly recognizable.

Many designs of abstract patterns of the 1980s found their inspiration in these remarkable Peruvian cloths.

⌒ Tribal Kilims ⌒

All over the Near East, and in India and parts of eastern Europe, kilims are woven. These pileless rugs are usually woven by the slit-tapestry technique, characterized by narrow slits between blocks of colour. The slit-tapestry

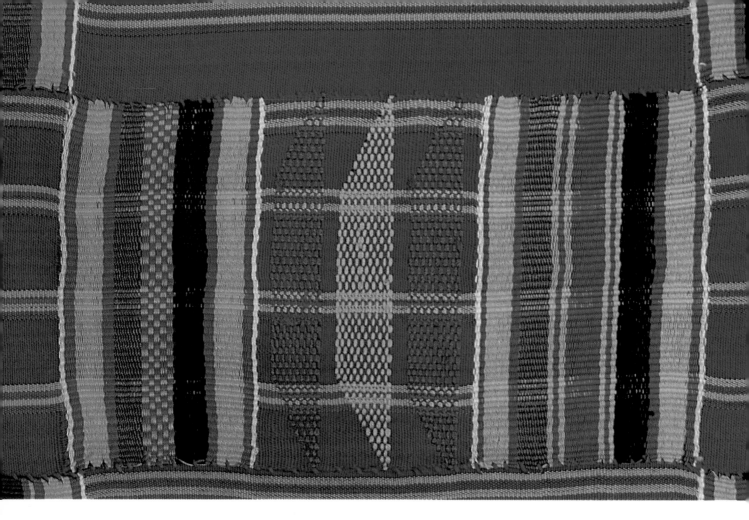

method is the most widespread technique for making rugs. Kilims are double-sided and almost identical on each side. In bold colours and simple geometric patterns such as diamonds, squares and checks, they are generally made from wool, though sometimes from cotton or silk.

Kilims are traditionally used as wall hangings, curtains or tent covers, since the slits prevent them from making really strong floor coverings. In India, they are known as dhurries.

∽ African Woven Geometrics ∾

In Africa narrow strip weaving is carried out on cotton or silk. Known as kente cloth, the fabric is patterned with stripes, often broken up by other geometric shapes. The strips are sewn together after weaving to form a staggering variety of designs and colourways. In 1977 Warners produced a collection called "Ethnic Origins" for which Graham Smith designed a screen-printed cotton entitled "Africa"; based on traditional African textiles, it has just such a patchwork of designs and patterns.

∽ Indian Abstracts ∾

In India, pattern is generally taken to mean the exquisite stylized natural forms that are so well known (see pages 126 and 146), but the Indians did also produce abstracts in which small patchwork-like squares were filled with floral motifs, small stripes and wavy lines. Cut-out appliqués included distorted elephant forms among indistinct vegetation. The ingenious ways in which these forms were used resulted in hundreds of different patterns and

African weaving is often done in strips on narrow looms and sewn together afterwards. The resulting kaleidoscope of stripes, broken by geometric brocaded shapes, is wonderfully varied, bright yet elegant; this cotton weave has an almost tartan quality. The colours are typical of those used in twentieth century African cloths.

designs. In sensitive but joyous colours, they are still very much in evidence in Indian fabrics today and can be obtained from importers of Indian textiles.

⌐ Chinese and Japanese Designs ⌐

Both the Chinese and the Japanese used appliqué and embroidery to create dragons and other objects which eventually became highly abstract. The lines were fluid and surprisingly informal, though following a set of very formal rules. The designs of Chinese tapestries were often too complicated for modern textiles, but individual motifs, such as waves, cloudlike designs or abstract forms of animals, are useful and interesting.

In Japan printed forms were created with stencils and paint, or resist-dyeing on cotton. Individual motifs were used in repeat, with geometric and floral patterns often alternating. Geometric heraldic motifs were much favoured.

Japanese designs were a popular source of inspiration at the time of the Aesthetic movement (see pages 44 and 156), and in 1870 Owen Jones produced the silk tissue design "Nipon". A century later, in the 1960s and '70s, there was again a fashion for Japanese-inspired abstracts, epitomized by "Ikebana" in black, white and grey by Barbara Brown for Heal Fabrics, and a number of other designs using motifs borrowed from Japan, such as circles, and cherry blossom in large repeats.

⌐ Ikat Patterns ⌐

The ikat technique is used all over the world but it was developed first in Indonesia, and was introduced to the West by the Dutch, who colonized the islands (then known as the Dutch East Indies). Ikats are woven from resist-dyed yarns, often creating patterns of symbolic importance and in a wide variety of designs.

The technique is to bind bundles of threads tightly together at chosen intervals along their length to create a pattern before the cloth is woven. Once dyed, the patterned warp sections are distributed across the loom to create the design. When weaving, the warp ends are set so closely together that they completely cover the weft, and so do not allow any spaces to interfere with the clarity of the design. The resulting outline has the characteristic faint fuzziness for which ikats have become so well known. The patterns can work horizontally or vertically, and simple or relatively complex patterns can be created by this method according to the alignment of the bound areas in the warp.

Indonesian weaving is highly individual, and it is possible to identify textile patterns from particular islands and even from specific regions of islands. The Indonesians believe that all animals and plants are invested with souls and all inanimate objects are endowed with spirits. Patterns commonly

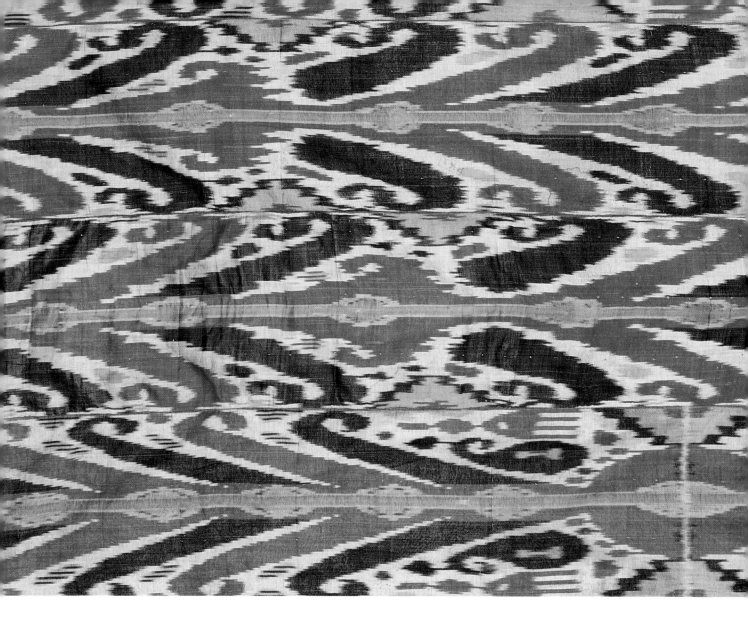

used include geometric shapes, as well as the pomegranate, the tree of life and the cypress tree, which are symbolic.

In north Borneo and Sarawak, anthropomorphic animal and abstract designs are squeezed into a central field between narrow stripes. Sometimes motifs are arranged in rows, and often various elements are placed in complex arrangements. Other Indonesian ikats range the motifs in rows of bright orange, midnight blue and black with semi-abstract sea-horses, deer, nude men and trees hung with skulls. In Indian ikats, the designs are mainly in narrow stripes with changing areas of colour, although the most complex are double ikats, or *patola*, with both warp and weft pre-dyed.

Japanese kasuri resist dyeing, which has become highly fashionable in the West in recent years, uses ikat techniques as well as many other ways of applying the dye. These include dip dyeing, plaiting the yarn, and weaving the material with added coarse yarn which is removed after dyeing. The patterns are entirely a result of this resist-dye work and are not due to any special kind of weaving. As well as realistic motifs, there are abstract patterns such as the traditional "mosquitoes" and "rice measure". Modern abstract compositions can consist of asymmetrical blocks of plain colour with blocks of checks or stripes.

Ikat is a dyeing technique used with different results all around the world. This ikat from central Asia includes the "pine" motif and brightly coloured straplike leaves sprouting from a central stem, all with the characteristic "fuzzy" outline.

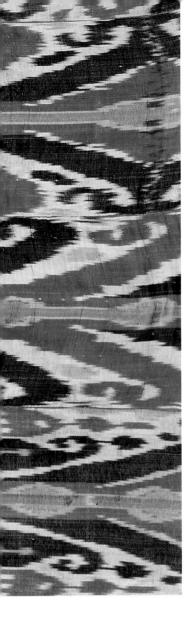

The simple, striped ikats, particularly those from India, have been an important influence in wallpaper and textile design of the 1980s.

⌐ Batik Patterns ⌐

Early batik has been found in the Far East, the Middle East, Central Asia and India. A resist-dyeing method, batik involves applying a "resist" such as liquid wax to a fabric to prevent it taking up the colour of the dyes.

Silk batiks from about AD 700 have been found in Japan. Made into screens, they are decorated with semi-abstract or stylized trees and animals, flute players, hunting scenes and stylized mountains. Probably the most accomplished batiks, however, come from Indonesia (formerly the Dutch East Indies). Specific areas of Indonesia have their own traditional patterns, which are easily recognizable. The brown, black and cream-coloured Kawung pattern comes from Central Java and is a very ancient design reflecting the belief in a universal structure.

A common Javanese motif is the "tumpal", a spear-like shape in which red, blue, black and cream are used, sometimes with gold for special fabrics.

Early in the nineteenth century attempts were made to develop machinery to produce cheaper imitations of batik prints, but it was difficult to match the local vegetable dyes, and the complex patterns required such a huge number of interlocking blocks that the cost was prohibitive. In the mid 1830s the Dutch did manage to establish several factories in Holland where attempts were made to produce batiks using the same methods as in the East Indies. East Indian craftsmen were employed and later the Dutch set up state-controlled combines in the East Indies, with each village specializing in a different craft. When the Swiss began to export imitation batik, the Javanese workshops responded by developing a form of wax block printing adapted from Indian techniques so that the Swiss could no longer compete.

In the early twentieth century the Germans developed tools and techniques for the mass production of batiks, which were used for furnishing and curtain fabrics. England at the same time perfected machine-printed batiks, principally for the African market. Some of these retained a certain amount of wax, producing semi-translucent effects of some charm. When the 1920s slump arrived, however, production ceased in Germany, and except for the so-called "Manchester batiks", the process once again fell to the traditional craftsmen in Indonesia or artist craftsmen in Europe.

The Dutch colonization of the Far East had led to museums being set up in the Dutch city of Haarlem, and the combined Javanese and Dutch traditions contributed significantly to Art Nouveau style (see page 129). The influence of batik can be seen in the work of people like Roger Fry of the Omega Workshop (see page 110), where Manchester "batiks" were also sold, and Charles Rennie Mackintosh (see page 133).

A small batik factory employing sixteen people was set up in Paris in 1916 by Madame Pangon, a batik artist of the Haarlem School. Another notable designer of the Haarlem School at around the same time was Chris Lebeau, whose intricate and delicate designs were used on screens and furniture inlays. At present there are a number of Javanese and European craftsmen producing batiks, both traditional and modern. In England Noel Dyrenforth is producing abstract batiks of a highly intricate and inventive nature, and "Manchester batiks" can still be obtained.

∽ Other Resist-dyed Designs ∽

Resist techniques are found in most of the regions of textile manufacture in Africa too, particularly in Nigeria and Senegal. The fabric may be tie-dyed, creating large and small circles which are given titles such as "big moons and little moons", "moons and stars" or "moons and fruits". Or before being dyed it may be painted with a resist of cassava paste in patterns such as scrolls, diagonally divided squares, diagonal stripes, "bow ties", herringbones, snakes and stylized flowers all combined in a patchwork-like design.

In parts of Nigeria the cotton fabric is stitched in patterns with raffia

ABOVE: This indigo-dyed Javanese cotton batik features a central medallion enclosed by paired geese along the edges and fan shapes in the corners. The greatest number of batik patterns comes from Java, and these in turn have derived from many places and periods, including India, China, Japan and, in modern times, Europe.

OVERLEAF: It was the Victorians who took tartan—originally used by the Scots for clothing—into their homes, where its rich colours and heavy texture suited their taste for respectable opulence. Here, the silk shawl (on the chair) and the silk wrap (on the dresser) are Victorian, and the rugs (bottom left) are antique, while the other tartans are modern.

before being dyed, and then may be burnished to a high sheen made possible by the excess indigo on the surface of the fabric. A cloth covered in squares, themselves filled with cross hatching, is called "cocoa". Another example, looking remarkably like a Snakes and Ladders board, has abstracted snakes, turtles, lions, crocodiles, birds or fish lurking on or between the squares. "Plantain" is a series of stitched columns with chevrons, while "fingers" is a pattern with a stitched eight-point star.

In Africa drawing and painting on cloth is thought to have developed in association with the conversion to Islam of the peoples of the southern Sahara. The technique has been adapted so that magical designs of Islamic origin appear within an overall pattern of small rectangles.

⌒ Checks, Plaids and Stripes ⌒

In the United States from the 1870s there was a growing interest in Americana. Document fabrics and papers, period rooms in museums and rebuilt colonial villages, traditional patchwork, stencilling, appliqué and embroidery patterns all contributed to the Early American style popular in the twentieth century, particularly since the 1950s. The 1976 Bicentenary reinforced the trend. The U.S. counterpart of the "English country house" look, the style features farmhouse or fine antique furniture; rag rugs, appliqué and patchwork quilts; ginghams, plaids, stripes, "toiles", muslins, printed calicoes and chintz; and soft furnishings edged with ruffles, scallops and/or piping.

Americans are used to combining checks, plaids or stripes and other patterns with great panache, juxtapositions which in some cases are only now being tried in Britain. In fact, in both Britain and the United States the 1980s brought a renewed interest in these simple geometrics, whether used singly or in bold combinations. The patterns are ideally suited to weaves because of their straight lines, and in spite of their simple patterns many variations and colourways are possible.

Ticking is a cotton or linen weave with narrow dark stripes in a cream ground. Traditionally used for covering feather mattresses and pillows, it is today produced in many colourways for curtains and upholstery. Some even incorporate tiny floral patterns woven into the stripes. More sophisticated weaves are created by using a wider palette of colours and different yarns, such as shot silk or viscose/cotton. Many autumnal reds, glaucous and deep greens and dusky purples are given a rich sheen by the use of these fibres, and a moiré effect is sometimes added.

Although some of the basic checked or striped cotton cloths imported from India in the eighteenth and early nineteenth centuries were known as ginghams, today gingham is taken to mean a simple cotton cloth woven from only two colours, one normally white, in balanced checks (with stripes of

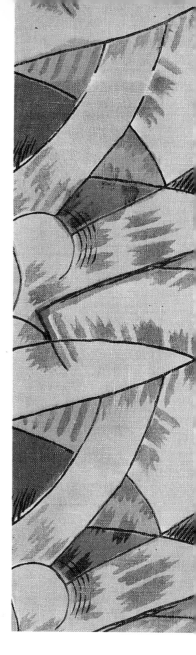

equal width in both directions). The traditional colours are white with red, green or blue but many other colourways are also available.

Madras is a traditional lightweight cotton fabric woven in India. It is thinner than gingham and sometimes includes viscose or other synthetic fibres with the cotton. Originally in black with red, it is now available in a wide range of plain and sateen weaves in very bright colours.

Tartan is a distinctive check weave pattern associated with Scottish Highland clans. Theoretically, tartans should be woven in the correct twill thread with a specific number of colours used in a particular order to make up patterns of precise size. However, outside Scotland, there are wide variations from these rules. Although originally woollen and intended for clothing (the term "plaid" actually meaning a kilt-length piece of tartan cloth), tartans are now widely used for furnishing and may be woven from silk as well as wool.

⌒ Rejecting the Status Quo ⌒

In Britain, early in the twentieth century there was a break from traditional designs and an effort to look for inspiration elsewhere.

The Omega Workshop, formed in 1913 by artist Roger Fry, set out to give people something fresh and different from the Arts and Crafts precepts (see pages 46 and 157). They decorated furniture, painted murals and panels and designed textiles, and, although the quality may sometimes have been a little amateurish, there was laudable energy and inventiveness and lots of colour. Omega lasted only seven years, but it left a permanent impression. Roger Fry and his co-directors Duncan Grant and Vanessa Bell all designed for the Workshop as did other artists of the time.

For their wall decorations, Duncan Grant and Vanessa Bell preferred to use the powder colours which could be bought at local hardware stores and mixed with size; they were available in a limited range of colours, which may account for some of the rather curious colourways. Duncan Grant's "Apollo and Daphne" and "Clouds" fabric designs of the 1930s catch the Omega quality well; Roger Fry's "Amenophis" was based on a still-life painting with a jug and eggs.

Grant and Bell provided an exhibit entitled "An Ideal Music Room" for the Alex Reid and Lefevre Gallery in 1932. A fabric called "Grapes", which upholstered a sofa and was made into curtains that ran along the whole of the end wall, was bought by Virginia Woolf for curtains and a sofa in her own home.

Long after Omega in 1981, a collection of furniture and textile designs by Memphis, a group of Italian designers led by Ettore Sotsass, was introduced at the Italian furniture fair and created a furore. Unlike Omega, Memphis wholeheartedly embraced mass production and modern materials like plastic. Yet in its rejection of the conventional, it echoed the Omega philosophy.

The Omega Workshop, in its seven years of existence, produced many energetic and original designs, often with unusual colourways. "Amenophis" is an Omega fabric designed by Roger Fry and printed on linen in France c. 1913.

Memphis provided a forum for avant-garde ideas, and its zany shapes, jagged edges and uncompromising colours influenced interior designs in Europe and America for a decade, especially through art colleges.

⟶ Links with Modern Abstract Art ⟵

Apart from the artists of the Omega Workshop, a number of other artists were working on printed textiles early in the twentieth century. The designs tended to be hand-blocked abstract or geometric repeats. The scale was governed by the size of the blocks, and the colours were usually subdued. Most of the artists believed in fostering greater harmony between modern architecture and abstract art, and their textiles were designed to be in keeping with the interiors of the time.

The French painter Raoul Dufy designed a number of block-printed textiles in the 1910s and 1920s, many of which had geometrical patterns influenced by the Cubists. Sonia Delauney, the Russian-born painter who lived in Paris from 1905, also produced many geometrically based textiles, wall hangings, carpets and other furnishings, as well as fashion fabrics and

theatre costumes. Her fabrics were characterized by strong colours, blocked shapes and lines.

After the First World War, Foxton's was the first firm to produce abstract artist-designed textiles in England, but the other firms that followed tended towards stylized patterns (see page 141). In 1937 Alastair Morton of Edinburgh Weavers succeeded in putting furnishing fabrics on the same level as painting and architecture when he introduced a range of subtle "Constructivist" fabrics designed by such artists as Ben Nicholson, Barbara Hepworth and Ashley Havinden.

Textiles designed by artists attracted more attention in the 1950s and early 1960s with the further development of screen printing, which has the unique ability to reproduce the painterly quality of these textiles, down to the last brush stroke. John Piper's "Chiesa della Salute", an abstract painting of a building, was a screen-printed satin rep designed for Sanderson around 1960.

The wallpaper manufacturer John Line's "Limited Editions 1951" were the first British screen-printed wallpapers and were commissioned from such well-known artists as John Minton, Jacqueline Groag, Lucienne Day and Sylvia Priestly. Many of the designs coordinated with cheaper, less obtrusive papers; the stronger design would often be used to accentuate one wall or as a panel, and the other would cover the rest of the walls. In the United States in the 1950s, screen-printed wallpaper panels based on designs by Matisse, Miró and Alexander Calder were developed. Among the most influential of American abstract-pattern designers was Angelo Testa, who in the 1940s and '50s created patterns based on juxtaposed rhythmic lines and mass.

Encouragement for artists to design fabric continued into the 1970s and '80s. In Britain in the early 1980s, the painter Howard Hodgkin was invited to design one of the room sets for an exhibition called "Four Rooms" at Liberty. He also designed two fabrics printed by Warners, a wavy stripe and a leopard print in blue, to go in the room set. In Philadelphia in 1979 the Fabric Workshop invited artists, architects and designers to develop printed fabrics in the workshops. Many interesting designs resulted, including Robert Venturi's "Signature" pattern for Knoll International and potter Richard DeVore's tablecloth, which was inspired by the crazing of one of his tall vases. Since then, a Hodgkin design has also been produced by Designers Guild, and the Fabric Workshop has continued its innovative projects.

⏤ Modernism and the Jazz Age ⏤

Modernist design (see page 49) was a 1920s phenomenon reflecting the need for gaiety in the post-war years, and many of the fabrics of that time were semi-abstract and "jazzy" in style. Arthur Sanderson & Sons, although today practically synonymous with floral designs, started selling fabrics under the Eton Rural Fabrics label in 1919. Before the First World War they had only

An abstract wallpaper showing the muted influence of Art Deco, produced by Sanderson in 1934.

produced wallcoverings, but the withdrawal of paper supplies for industry during the war had resolved Sandersons to diversify. The first designs were a riot of semi-abstract patterns, with clashing colours and bold combinations of natural and geometric forms. They were described by one reviewer as "magnificent Jazz designs with stripes and broken arrangements of orange and black, glimmering blue and gold, and rich crimson, treated with all the harmonious freedom and abandonment which is Jazz." Later collections included stylized plant forms (see page 139). The Eton Rural Fabrics had the contemporary feeling people were hungering for, satisfying the need for exuberance and free expression after the self-denial of the war.

⌒ Art Deco: Deliberately Outrageous ⌒

The Art Deco style of the 1920s and 1930s was another manifestation of the "Jazz Age". A reaction against the undulating lines of Art Nouveau (see page 129), it has been called "domesticated Cubism" and was characterized by solid, rectilinear shapes. Noted for its bold, flat motifs which were often geometric or naïvely drawn, its flashes of sharp colour and flamboyant patterns, Art Deco was not a movement but a style that emerged gradually.

The origins of Art Deco go back to the early years of the century, when Matisse and the other Fauves were advocating the use of assertive colours and strong patterns in painting, and when the brilliant set designs of the Ballets Russes were the talk of Paris. The Cubists introduced African influences and a geometric breaking up of forms, contributing to the growing interest in abstract pattern. Egyptian motifs and the Mayan and Aztec art of Central America were also sources of inspiration. Recurring Art Deco motifs are the stepped ziggurat shape of Aztec temples, chevrons and geometric shapes such as the circle, semicircle, triangle, octagon and cube.

Art Deco took its name from the Paris Exhibition of 1925—the Exposition Internationale des Arts Décoratifs et Industriels Modernes—which was its definitive launch pad as a populist style. Although Art Deco in its purest, and most outrageous, form was largely restricted to the wealthy and avant-garde, it was an important source of popular design in the 1920s and 1930s, especially in the United States. In the 1960s it became fashionable once more; for example, "Archway" by Eddie Squires, a 1968 screen-printed cotton, was inspired by 1930s cinema architecture. In fact, Art Deco has been an ingredient of almost all Post-Modern design since the 1960s, showing its influence in simplified variations of the original ideas.

⌒ Avant-garde Design of the 1950s and '60s ⌒

Geometric patterns, many of them heavily influenced by Op Art (a style of art using special optical effects), were popular in the 1950s and '60s, and the '50s was also the time when the fashion for abstract designs was at its height, though most of these were commissioned for modern public buildings rather than private homes.

The 1951 Festival of Britain, which coincided with the greater recognition of freelance textile designers in Britain, helped encourage manufacturers to try out new designs in a modern style. Heals Fabrics Ltd were one of the pioneering manufacturers who encouraged and promoted adventurous young designers. The award-winning "Calyx", a screen-printed linen, was designed by Lucienne Day (the foremost English pattern designer of the 1950s and '60s) for Heals. The "Calyx" bell shapes, linked by stick-like lines, were based on an abstraction of naturalistic floral images and epitomized the new look for furnishings of the post-war period, in many ways capturing the spirit of the age. ("Calyx" was also widely used in America, where it was distributed by Greeff Fabrics Inc.)

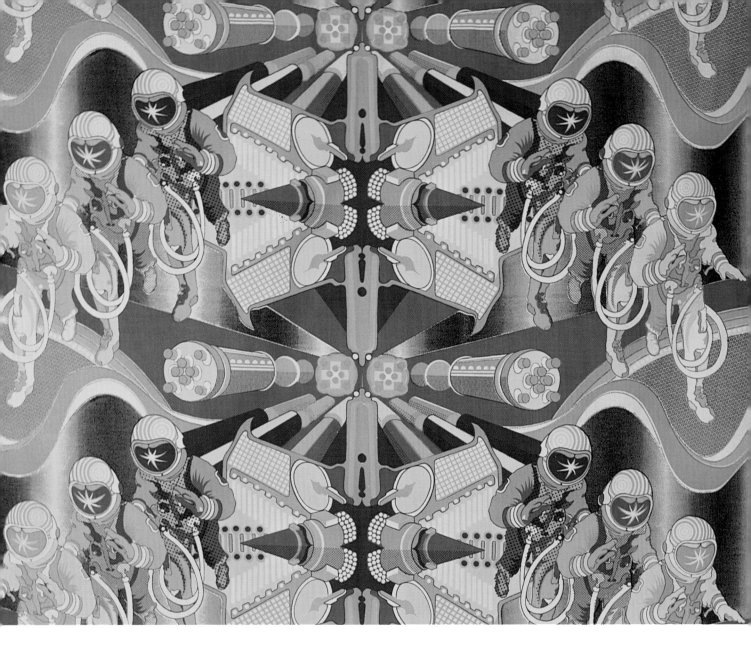

Warners, under the design directorship of Eddie Squires, made good use of the creative mood of the 1960s, producing a constant supply of innovative furnishing cottons by talented young designers. "Space Walk" by Sue Palmer was a screen-printed cotton inspired by the first men on the moon.

Barbara Brown designed for Heals many large, bright Op Art patterns involving cubes, rods and lots of red and black or black and white. Shirley Craven's designs for Hull Traders were equally bold, with large-scale repeats and a feeling of movement. Other avant-garde manufacturers included Edinburgh Weavers under Alastair Morton, Conran Fabrics, Tibor Reich, Liberty, Warners, David Whitehead, Cavendish Textiles and Tamesa.

⟍ Technological Inspiration ⟋

A group of textile designs, the "Festival Patterns" which were devised specifically for the 1951 Festival of Britain, had a major influence on 1950s design. Reflecting the prevailing interest in patterns drawn from science and technology, they were based on the patterns formed by crystal structures seen under a microscope. For example, Marianne Straub's "Helmsley", designed for Warner and Sons, was a Jacquard weave based on the structure of nylon. Even the curtains of the Regatta Restaurant at the Festival were in a pattern based on crystallography designed by Marianne Straub. Also used in the restaurant was a design by Alec Hunter inspired by china clay seen

ABOVE: "Forum",
designed in 1989 by
Fujiwo Ishimoto for
Marimekko, epitomizes
Scandinavian twentieth-
century design.

LEFT: Lucienne Day's
award-winning "Calyx"
design was first produced
by Heal Fabrics in 1951.
Like so much design of
the period, its abstract
shapes took a new look at
everyday forms.

through a microscope. Other abstract designs of the 1950s and '60s were
drawn from electronics and engineering, mathematical symbols and scientific
notation, and scientific advances of the day.

In the 1960s under the design directorship of Eddie Squires, Warner &
Sons developed a "technological" abstract style very much their own.
Squires's "Colourtron", of 1967, named after a device used in colour
television, was based on a silicon circuit. "Space Walk", designed by Sue
Palmer in 1969, for Warners, was a screen-printed cotton depicting astro-
nauts on the Moon. Her "Isometric", designed in 1968 for Warners, was
inspired by opticians' colour charts and gave a three-dimensional effect.

In 1967 Eduardo Paolozzi was commissioned by Manchester's Whitworth
Art Gallery to design the "Whitworth Tapestry", which marked the official
opening of the newly modernized gallery. Woven under Archie Brennan at
the Dovecot Studios of the Edinburgh Tapestry Company, Paolozzi's design
was based on a series of ten screen-prints entitled "Universal Electronic
Vacuum" which explored popular culture and computer technology. It
consisted of squares and oblongs filled with squares, stripes, mosaic and

other forms in reds, blues and yellows and anticipated his later mosaic designs for Tottenham Court Road Underground Station in London.

⌒ Pop Art Imagery ⌒

In the 1960s and '70s there was continual experimentation and revolt against hitherto established rules. The "Palladio 8" range produced by Sanderson, for example, was much influenced by the Pop Art movement. It was aimed at an affluent consumer who was prepared to explore and exploit all forms of graphic and three-dimensional design. Its imagery was culled from various sources including Art Nouveau, Art Deco, Op Art and psychedelic drugs. Often these were patterns with recognizable antecedents, but in a very different guise and in much brasher colours. Typical of the time were the blocklike forms of Margo Fabrics' "Brix" collection curtain material, which was especially favoured by architects.

Fiorucci in Italy came to symbolize the avant-garde with his "junky chic" artefacts and mass-market fabrics aimed at the young. His fabric prints were in acid colours covered in small explosions of restless patterns. Geometric shapes were used, but without the formal discipline of traditional designs.

Wallpaper manufacturers tended to stick to simple dot, stripe and asterisk motifs, which were unobtrusive in both shape and colour.

⌒ Scandinavian Textiles ⌒

Some of the fabrics of Sweden's "Group of Ten"—which was formed in the 1970s—also explored designs that were derived from Pop Art. Their first collection, which appeared in 1972, aimed for lasting, rather than actually fashionable, design. They use strong, uninhibited colours and bold patterns.

Scandinavian design of the twentieth century has always been confident, simple and bright, using stripes, broken stripes and geometrics in bold planes of colour, well suited to a harsh climate and many months of darkness. In Finland Marimekko have been designing bright, bold, unmistakable fabrics since the 1960s. Marimekko's identity is so strong that the styles of individual designers can be incorporated without concealing it. Vuoko Eskolin-Nurmesniemi, chief designer at Marimekko, set up on her own in 1964. Like Marimekko, her firm, Vuoko, is known for its colours and patterns combining subtle adaptations of Finnish rustic traditions with fresh, uninhibited colours and simplicity of form.

⌒ Abstract Textile Prints of the 1980s and '90s ⌒

In the 1980s Susan Collier and Sarah Campbell of the British design team Collier Campbell (see page 142) produced some very successful abstract prints in bold colours, many of them inspired by painters such as Dufy and Matisse. Later in the decade, Osborne & Little's "Bizarre" collection

A selection of Collier Campbell designs. (Clockwise from top left) "Cote d'Azure" fabric, "Tambourine" bed linen, "Guitar" fabric, "Tiger Circus" wool shawl, "Birdsong" fabric, "Bauhaus" fabric for Liberty, and "Sakkara City" fabric for Habitat.

launched a completely new look. Based on the strangely exotic patterns of early eighteenth-century bizarre silks, it featured abstract motifs superimposed on plaids and checks. Their "Romagne" collection also incorporated abstract motifs that creatively interpreted the past, in this case the Renaissance, with medallions, stars, sunbursts, and chequered diamonds.

The American designer Jack Lenor Larsen has worked closely with ethnic weaving communities all over the world and translates the qualities of their designs into machine-made weaves and prints. Also in the United States, Ben Rose produces satin silk damasks of great subtlety and splendour.

Gustav and Carla Kindermann design coordinated rayon and cotton ranges for Atelier Druck Kindermann KG in Austria with painterly strokes and colours. The fabrics are screen printed with dye for the colour areas and with a chemical liquid which expands after printing to create raised outlines.

Gianni Versace's stylish bold patterns are produced by Christian Fischbacher in Switzerland. Also in Switzerland, Team Creation Baumann have used machine stitching to produce luxurious effects and pleats in curtain fabrics.

Esteban Figuerola SA, the Spanish company, produces the richest of abstract patterns using lacquer printing, in which the printed colour may be augmented with fine metallic powders on opalescent crystals (sometimes from ground-up seashells, as used for some of the early flock wallpapers).

Shyam Ahuja in Bombay produces very beautiful cotton and silk ribbed weaves which are strongly but subtly coloured. The American Jim Thompson, through his firm in Thailand, produces sumptuous silks, including silk ikats, in glowing shades.

Throughout the twentieth century, abstract patterns have remained an essential element in modern (and post-modern) interiors, since they enhance the sculptural nature of chairs, show off the effect of designer lighting and yet provide a visual interest of their own.

RIGHT: For over three decades the American Jim Thompson has had working links with Thailand, where the company he founded produces sumptuous but exceedingly subtle woven silks, including ikats and slub weaves. This range of red and green silk weaves gives an indication of the variety, quality and style of Thompson designs.

CHAPTER FIVE

STYLIZED DESIGNS

"...every outline...must be full of life and motion so as
to delight the eye by its diversity."

GEORGES FARCY, Art Nouveau architect, c. 1900

Stylized designs can be defined as those based on recognizable images which have been ordered or arranged so that the pattern becomes more dominant than its individual parts. These patterns take many forms and can be categorized in many ways. The categories included in this book are simply a convenient way of looking at the patterns, their sources and their treatment through the many vicissitudes of fashion. Some patterns will inevitably overlap into other categories, but designs can never be tidily put away in boxes. Examining patterns from more than one angle gives a more complete picture.

Small Repeat Patterns

Small-scale repeat patterns are perennially popular. They look fresh and pretty, they never dominate, and they are unlikely to clash with other colours or patterns. Consisting of one or more isolated shapes repeating (most often in diagonal lines) over the whole fabric or wallpaper, they tend to form a textural effect when viewed from a distance. Common motifs include stylized fruit, flowers, foliage, heraldic devices and simple geometric shapes.

Islamic textiles of the Middle East and northern Africa feature a large repertoire of these small overall patterns, many highly stylized floral motifs.

Small-patterned wallpapers, particularly sprigged papers, were popular in Regency Britain, many of them with a pin-dot ground. At around the same

This nineteenth-century block-printed cotton was found backing an embroidered prayer mat from Persia. Its small, stylized overall pattern—featuring the "pine" (paisley) motif, made up of tiny flowers and leaves—is typical of Islamic textiles of the Middle East and North Africa.

time there was a fashion for Indian-style printed cottons with detailed infills within each pattern, frequently with a sharp yellow ground. Small printed patterns were often used as fillings for borders. Their stars, seaweed-like motifs and stylized leaves and flowers were probably imitations of woven patterns.

Silks have been patterned with small motifs from the sixteenth century. During the late Victorian era the Aesthetic movement and fashion for Japanese-style decoration (see pages 44 and 155) led to the production in Britain and the United States of silks patterned with small Japanese-style prints. These were often incorporated into roller prints, for which their small scale made them well suited. Motifs included stylized birds, insects, blossoms and patterned circles arranged almost like patchwork. From 1850 to 1880 the silk firms Charles Norris & Company, Daniel Walters & Sons and, from 1870, Warners produced woven silk damasks and damasquettes with satin and rep figuring, in the form of stylized bunches of flowers on dark backgrounds. Some were very intricate, with undulating stems delicately connecting detailed leaves and flowers. Motifs might sit alone on the ground, or they might be framed by diagonal or curved lines.

During the second half of the twentieth century, "Americana" (see page 107) designs took their inspiration from document fabrics and wallpapers and other decorative arts, particularly stencilled patterns, patchwork and appliqué. Many of these fabrics and papers feature small-scale stylized patterns, such as the small, all-over "calico" prints, which coordinate with larger-scale designs. Schumacher, Brunschwig & Fils and Greeff Fabrics each contributed to the naive document style.

Corresponding to the well-established U.S. interest in Americana, in England the 1970s brought a major revival of the small, stylized patterns of the early nineteenth century, epitomized by Laura Ashley's furnishing fabrics and wallpapers. From small beginnings in the 1950s—designing tea towels in her kitchen which were produced by Laura's husband Bernard—grew the Laura Ashley empire. The firm made its name initially with its one-colour tiny floral prints and its very English flavour.

As well as Laura Ashley, the design companies Designers Guild (founded by Tricia Guild in 1970) and Osborne & Little (founded by Peter Osborne and Antony Little in 1968) have included many small stylized prints in their ranges of fabrics and papers. Small prints also appear in most low-priced wallpaper and textile ranges today.

The badge and cipher of Edward I as Prince of Wales, seen in a 16th century stained glass window, became widely used in neo-Gothic textile designs.

⌒ Classical Ornament ⌒

Much of the Western style of interior decoration is derived from ancient Greece by way of Rome. Classical styles based on Greek and Roman forms and mathematical laws of proportion applied not only to architecture and

The nineteenth-century architect A W N Pugin designed this wallpaper for London's Houses of Parliament. Its Tudor roses, medieval portcullis and VR (Victoria Regina) monogram are typical of the heraldic motifs he used in his Gothic Revival wallpapers. It was block printed by S Scott for J G Crace, with whom Pugin collaborated on many wallpapers.

fine art but to interior decoration too. The discovery of the Golden House of Nero in around 1500 and the excavations at Pompeii and Herculaneum in the eighteenth century have contributed much to what is known about Classical interiors.

Roman decorative themes became part of the vocabulary of Classical ornament that was used in the Renaissance and in Classical revivals thereafter. These include such stylized motifs as the acanthus leaf; vine leaf and grapes; palmette; ivy, laurel, olive and anthemion; festoon and garland; rosette; the human mask surrounded by foliage; putti (cupids); the egg-and-dart pattern; and "grotesques" (see page 137).

⌒ Heraldic Motifs ⌒

From the thirteenth century, heraldic devices played an increasingly important part in the decoration of homes. Shields and coats of arms were painted on to walls, incorporated in stained glass and plate, and woven into wall hangings and tapestries. The simple shapes and colours of these early coats of arms and crests made them well suited to repeat patterns. In the sixteenth century, heraldic devices appeared on wainscot panels, leather hangings and on the first wallpaper panels, block printed in black and white.

A paper, c. 1550, found adhering to a wattle-and-daub wall in Worcestershire, England, contains the arms of England (lions, fleurs de lys), Tudor roses, vases of flowers and masks. A variation of this paper has been found with St George and the dragon in place of the masks. Other heraldic motifs found on wallpapers of the time include a portcullis, the lion and unicorn, and the Prince of Wales feathers.

Heraldry was a distinctive feature of the sixteenth-century linen damasks woven in the Flemish towns of Ghent, Courtrai, Oudenaarde and Ypres. Motifs included the shields of St George and of England and France, crowns, Tudor roses, and animals such as dogs, rats, dragons and seahorses.

In the late eighteenth century, the stained glass windows of "Gothick" homes (see page 95) often incorporated heraldic devices. A number of Pugin's Gothic-style wallpapers (see page 95) of the mid-nineteenth century—such as the papers he designed for London's new Palace of Westminster (1843) and Houses of Parliament (1847)—included heraldic motifs with crowns, fleurs de lys, monograms and national emblems. In 1887 William Morris—who advocated a return to medieval design—designed a wallpaper with crowns and thistles and the initials VRI, for Balmoral Castle. In the twentieth century, John Line & Sons produced a wallpaper trellis design for Windsor Castle incorporating the monogram of George VI.

⌒ Paisley Patterns ⌒

The exotic paisley pattern derived from twill-woven shawls made from the wool of Kashmiri goats in India from the fifteenth century and imported into Europe in the eighteenth century. The highly stylized floral patterns were widely used in Mogul art. The familiar comma-shaped "pine" motif is thought to have been based on illustrations of the growing shoot of the date palm, which appeared on European herbals imported into India.

The popularity and relative scarcity of the imported shawls encouraged European weavers to produce woven silk shawls imitating the Kasmiri, or "cashmere", shawls, from the late eighteenth century. Norwich, Edinburgh and the Spitalfields area of London were the main centres of production initially. During the nineteenth century, Lyon and Vienna also began weaving the shawls, and Paisley, in Scotland, became a major manufacturer, giving its name to the pattern. But it was France which led the way in design and which invented the Jacquard loom (see page 19), making possible faster, more complex weaving. The European shawls nearly equalled the Kashmiri shawls in beauty of colour and technical quality, and they were exported to other European countries and also the United States.

As printed paisleys were faster and less expensive to produce than woven

Indian Kashmiri, or "cashmere", shawls incorporating the "pine" (paisley) motif were imported into England from the eighteenth century. They were much coveted for their luxurious softness and intricate woven patterns, such as seen here in a portion of a shawl woven in Kashmir c. 1830.

ones, many of the European shawls were block printed on cotton or silk gauze. Sometimes the patterns were so exactly simulated that they even contained tiny lines in imitation of the original twill weave. By the end of the nineteenth century, block printing had been replaced by roller printing. America was printing its own paisley shawls by this time, too.

Umritza cashmere was one of Liberty of London's early triumphs. Arthur Liberty, realizing that the Indian cashmere shawls would not wear well, worked with English weavers and eventually succeeded in producing a fabric which was soft, supple, light and warm. Introduced in 1879, the shawls were produced in neutral tints and also in "all the art colours" (see page 44).

Today's printed paisley fabrics, with their rich hues and stylized motifs, usually set against a vibrant ground, are very similar to the original Kashmiri and European patterns, and the paisley motif has been used in hundreds of different variations on printed textiles throughout the world.

⟶ Provençal Prints ⟵

The bright, multicoloured prints of Provence are familiar all over the world. The stylized patterns—mainly floral, geometric or paisley—are printed in strong, vividly contrasting colours, such as tomato red and saffron yellow, evoking the sunny landscape of Provence. Their history goes back four centuries.

In the late sixteenth century, painted and printed calicoes from India (see page 146) were imported into Marseilles. The inhabitants of the region were greatly beguiled by these *indiennes*, as they called them, and set about mastering the traditional Oriental skills of printing on to cotton. The manufacture of *indiennes* was prohibited in France to protect the indigenous weaving industry, but Marseilles and Avignon were outside French jurisdiction, being part of a papal state. By the mid-seventeenth century, the Indian prints had proved resoundingly successful, upsetting the traditional French textiles industry, and leading to a ban on their importation into France. Marseilles and Avignon were able to continue production, but only for local consumption and foreign trade. A thriving black market operated, and in 1759, when the ban was dropped, many workshops were still in existence and could benefit from the new freedom. In the nineteenth century, many designs were actually inspired by the patterns of the Jouy printworks (see page 174). However, most of the workshops—which block printed the cottons using vegetable dyes—were unable to compete with automation.

Today, Provençal-based firms such as Souleiado and Les Olivades use original pear wood blocks as the basis of their modern screen prints. Although they now use synthetic dyes, the colours are kept as near as possible to those of the traditional vegetable dyes.

Modern Provençal prints typically have small, regularly spaced motifs

such as stylized daisies, leaves, stars or *botehs* (the paisley, or pine, motifs that
are a legacy from the prints' origins in the Mogul art of India) on a
background that is vividly coloured or, occasionally, white. Sometimes the
motifs are organized into stripes or borders. Other prints feature all-over
patterns of stylized flowers and leaves linked by tendril-like stems.

⌒ Art Nouveau Designs ⌒

Art Nouveau, with its flowing lines within a linear framework, was a
decorative movement of great vitality. It flourished on the Continent from
around 1890 to 1905, reaching its climax at the Paris Universal Exhibition of
1900. Although in France, Belgium, Italy, Spain, Germany and Austria it
embraced architecture and all aspects of interiors, in Britain and America,
apart from the illustrations of Aubrey Beardsley, it really only affected the
decorative arts, particularly wallcoverings and tiles, textiles, wrought ironwork, glass and jewellery.

SAVON "LE CHAT"

Art Nouveau patterns are still popular for fabrics and wallpapers. The wallpaper and border shown here are "Astrid" and "Atheneum" by Cole & Son, and the fabric on the table is a woven version of the famous Liberty print "Hera".

Art Nouveau artists favoured elegance, beauty and decorativeness. Rejecting naturalism, they wished instead to capture the essence of nature. On the Continent, Art Nouveau developed into a fully fledged, extravagantly curvilinear style based on writhing arabesque forms. Graceful plant forms provided the principal motifs, and the intricate designs were characterized by a great freedom and fluidity. In Britain there was the same emphasis on line — either as outlines or as sinuous stems, entwining tendrils and plants (especially roses), blossoming branches and exquisitely curved knots — but these meandering lines tended to be combined with strong vertical lines. The Scottish architect Charles Rennie Mackintosh and his Glasgow School pioneered this more severe form of Art Nouveau but had more impact on the Continent than in Britain or America. In particular, Mackintosh was a major influence in the "Jugendstil" version of Art Nouveau developed in Vienna by artists of the Wiener Werkstätte (an arts and crafts centre founded in 1903, and directed by the German architect Josef Hoffmann). The work of the Wiener Werkstätte in turn inspired many modern textile designs, particularly small geometric and abstract floral prints.

The designer Louis C Tiffany was largely responsible for the growth of Art Nouveau in America. In Britain the Silver Studio (founded in 1880 by Arthur Silver and continued by his son Rex), Harry Napper (who also worked for the Silver Studio for a time) and the architect C F A Voysey were among those who produced many textile patterns in the full-blown style, but these were mainly for Continental, Scottish and American manufacturers; relatively few Art Nouveau fabrics were actually produced in England. Typical Art Nouveau textile patterns were complex and elongated, incorporating curved, intertwined flowers such as tulips, poppies or lilies, as well as shells, butterflies or peacock feathers. Rex Silver, Voysey and Napper were among the designers who produced wallpapers in the Art Nouveau style.

Art Nouveau grew out of the Arts and Crafts movement (see pages 46 and 158), in which the characteristic curvilinear shapes could already be seen in wallpapers, fabrics and illustration. The Scottish architect, A H Mackmurdo — who in 1882 founded the Century Guild, an Arts and Crafts offshoot — had a taste for flowing forms which anticipated Art Nouveau. One of his book illustrations, published in 1883, is thought to be the earliest example of Art Nouveau design. The basic characteristic of the style can also be seen in Mackmurdo's wallpaper designs of stylized, rather grandiose leaf and butterfly shapes.

Apart from the Arts and Crafts movement, other influences in the development of Art Nouveau were Japanese art, the Rococo style and Celtic designs (see pages 155, 35 and 94 respectively).

The name "Art Nouveau" came from a Parisian shop, L'Art Nouveau, specializing in modern design. The Italians, however, called the style "Stile

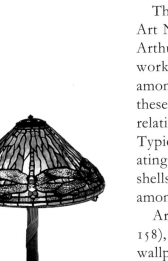

Tiffany Studios' stained glass strongly influenced Art Nouveau design. The "Dragonfly" table lamp has the required wavy lines and the glowing blues and greens.

Liberty", after the London shop, which sold Art Nouveau silver, jewellery and textiles. Liberty Art Nouveau furnishing fabrics were commissioned from many artists, including Voysey, Lindsay P Butterfield, Frank Miles, Sidney Mawson, Arthur Willshaw, Edgar L Pattison, J M Doran, Jessie M King and Arthur Wilcock. Wilcock's "Daffodils and Crocus" chintz was bought by the illustrator Walter Crane for his own dining room.

⌒ Wallpaper Frieze Patterns ⌒

Coinciding with the Art Nouveau style was the vogue for deep wallpaper friezes, which were popular in Britain from the mid 1890s until around 1910. Art Nouveau motifs featured in many of these friezes, particularly those of

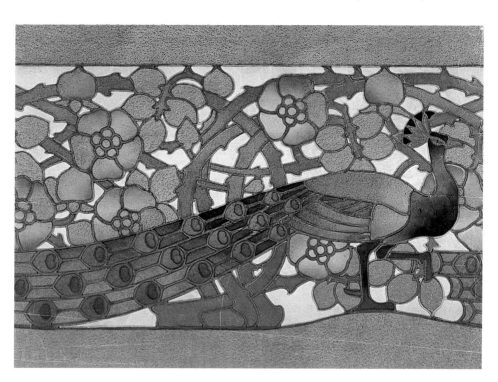

William Shand Kydd (see page 83), a leading manufacturer. Although they might be as deep as 90–120 cm/3–4 feet, most friezes were 50 cm/21 inches in depth, which was the standard width of a roll of wallpaper. The outlines were hand blocked and the colour applied by stencil. Many featured delicate blended and stippled effects and hand gilding.

The most common subject matter was stylized flowers and foliage, but allegorical scenes, landscapes and seascapes also featured. The friezes were used throughout the home, with different patterns considered suitable for each room. A floral frieze in delicate colours might be used in the drawing room, one with deeper, richer colours in the dining room, and a frieze

featuring sporting motifs in the billiard room. Bedrooms and ladies' boudoirs were usually given narrow, more subtle friezes, especially floral. There were also many nursery friezes, some of them designed by well-known children's book illustrators. Motifs depicted, for example, "seaside joys, nursery heroes and the pleasures and pastimes of winter", as well as Boy Scouts and the drawings of Beatrix Potter. The friezes were the work of a variety of designers, including the Silver Studio, Lindsay Butterfield, Walter Crane, William Neatby and William Shand Kydd himself.

With Empire undertones, the horizontal alignment of Walter Crane's "Fruit Frieze", hand printed in 1903, was ideally suited for running along a wall above the picture rail.

⌒ Washable Wallpaper ⌒

Washable wallpapers (see page 83) were introduced in England in the second half of the nineteenth century and remained popular into the twentieth century. Known as Sanatories, they were characterized by their slightly brownish colour, and designs were created that would be in keeping with this. In the 1890s Arthur Gwatkin designed rococo leaf shapes specifically for Sanatories that would be used in halls and on staircases; they were manufactured by Wyllie & Lochhead. Christopher Dresser—botanist and designer extraordinaire of everything from textiles and wallpaper to pottery and wrought iron, who collaborated with Owen Jones on *The Grammar of Ornament* (see page 89)—designed many Sanatories. These featured angular, stylized birds and plants, often in tile-effect geometric frameworks. The

Silver Studio also produced designs for Sanatories in such patterns as stylized tulips alternating with leaves to create a tile effect.

⸺ Leatherwork Wallpapers ⸺

In the late nineteenth century, embossed and gilded wallpapers imitating Cordovan and Japanese leather hangings became very fashionable, particularly for dadoes. (Richly patterned embossed and gilded leather—introduced to Europe by the Islamic peoples of North Africa after the Moorish invasion of Spain—had been used extensively as wallhangings from the sixteenth until the eighteenth century. The leather hangings either illustrated a story or used heraldic emblems or "Grotesque" ornament—which combined incongruous human and animal figures with scrolls, foliage, urns of flowers, etc.—in repetitive patterns.)

At London's Victoria & Albert Museum there is a roll of unused wallpaper with a fruit-and-floral pattern within ogival borders that simulates a seventeenth-century Spanish leather hanging, probably of the type known as Cordelova; it was embossed, silvered, hand coloured and then varnished. In the United States M H Birge was producing imitations of leatherwork using embossed paper in various sizes. Patterns in the very intricate leather texturing included baskets of flowers, heraldic motifs and unashamedly Art Nouveau designs.

Sanderson sold "leather" wallpapers in either the Spanish or the Japanese style. The Spanish type was heavier and used Classical motifs, while the Japanese type featured more colour, particularly a glowing, ember-like red. Liberty, who at that time specialized in Japanese-style decoration, was one of the major retailers of these papers. Printed from woodblocks, the Japanese papers had such designs as grasses and fans in gold on a red ground, birds, peacock feathers, pineapples, orchids and foliage, painted in red and gold. Many leather-effect wallpapers were printed in Japan to British designs by such firms as Alexander Rottmann's.

⸺ Stylized Design of the 1920s and '30s ⸺

Although the Art Deco style (see pages 50 and 113), which was taken up by the avant-garde of the 1920s and '30s, was based on abstract geometric shapes, many stylized motifs also characterized the style. Sunbursts, fans, hills and clouds, fountains, stylized trees and flowers, and animal forms, particularly the deer and ibex, were all common Art Deco motifs. Patterns were full of broken geometric shapes and lines, with small floral sprigs scattered about.

There was a short Art Deco revival in the early 1960s. At that time, Martin Battersby's fabrics (inspired by the French designers Bakst and Poiret) and Bernard Neville's stylized shocking-pink and orange cabbage roses on a

LEFT: "Tulips and Daffodils", produced in 1922–3, was typical of the vividly coloured stylized patterns of many of Sanderson's early Eton Rural Fabrics range.

RIGHT: "Boating" was a cretonne produced in 1931 under Sanderson's Eton Rural Fabrics label. Manufacturers of Modernist patterns such as this were hard hit by the depression and consequent conservatism of the 1930s, and the label was withdrawn in 1936.

green and black wavy ground were both designed for Liberty. In 1990 Liberty produced two further prints, "Melbourne" and "Cranbourne", based on Art Deco, and specifically but loosely on ceramic designs by the Art Deco ceramics designers Clarice Cliff and Susie Cooper.

The Eton Rural Fabrics range of the 1920s and early '30s featured not only semi-abstract patterns (see page 112) but also stylized plant forms, such as daffodils, tulips, crocuses, nasturtiums and hyacinths, all in exciting combinations of glowing colour. The Eton Rural Fabrics label was withdrawn in

1936 after Modernist patterns and primary hues fell out of fashion, but a limited number of the fabrics were sold in the late 1980s by Sanderson. Other firms, such as Warners and Designers Guild, have also recently introduced casually stylized patterns with strong undertones of the interwar years.

∼ Constructivist Influences ∼

In the 1930s England produced textiles based on stylized, compressed scenes such as "Welwyn Garden City", a block print by Doris Gregg, which was exhibited at the Metropolitan Museum of Art in New York in 1930. Welwyn Garden City was one of the purpose-built British "new towns", and the print shows it from an aerial view. Other designers, including the Americans Marion Dorn (working in England) and Ruth Reeves, also designed scenes viewed from above, as seen in much Futurist and Constructivist art.

In Russia in the early 1920s artists such as Liubov, Popova, Stepanova, Burylin and Griun produced many Constructivist designs for textiles, the philosophy being, in a nutshell, that art was bourgeois and hypocritical but that industrial design reflected the needs and efforts of the people. Textiles

Liberty's "Cranbourne" fabric is part of a range introduced in 1990 which recreates the mood of 1930s textiles, though the colours are softer than the Art Deco originals.

provided an ideal way to marry abstract form to social use, to turn art into production. They rejected the geometric motif in favour of symbolic images.

The first post-Revolution cottons were decorated with Soviet symbols such as the hammer and sickle and red stars, as well as everyday tools and tools for industry. Artists were trying to make fabric express the ideas of the revolution, and popular themes included "The Demonstration", "The Tractor", "Electrification", "Pioneers" and "Factories".

These designs varied from standard production in such aspects as colour, execution, number of rollers used and variety of ornamental elements. Some cotton prints were designed in the French Classical manner, interspersing traditional roses or stripes not with the usual florets or leaves but with tiny aeroplanes or exploding fireworks.

⌐ Marrying the Fine and Applied Arts ⌐

Harold Sanderson, the textile and wallpaper manufacturer, suggested in 1933 that art should be brought into manufacture. He thought it would not only improve the nation's finances but also bring fresh life and new thinking into fabric designs and "raise life to a higher ethical plane". (In fact, it was not entirely a new idea. In the eighteenth century, the French wallpaper manufacturer Réveillon had employed many talented artists. In the late nineteenth century, Jeffrey & Company of Great Britain and Warren Fuller of the United States had commissioned leading architects, artists and illustrators to design wallpaper for them. Also, a number of architects, from A W N Pugin and Owen Jones onwards, had created wallpapers and textiles, often for their own buildings.) Art was associated with good taste, and artists were acknowledged to have greater visual awareness. Architects, too, were looking for fabrics which would suit streamlined modern architecture (see page 49).

By the mid 1930s–1940s, a few progressive companies were commissioning artists to design for them, and many of the resulting designs were highly stylized. Tom Heron of Cresta Silks, Alastair Morton of Edinburgh Weavers, Allan Walton and Zika Ascher were all convinced that they could supply customers with a superior product if a fine artist were involved in its production. The sculptor Henry Moore produced a few designs, such as "Reclining Figure", a screen-printed linen wall hanging for Zika Ascher in 1948. Since Moore's drawings were in wax crayons and watercolour, Ascher used a wax-resist technique to print them; it took many months to get satisfactory results. Moore's designs work well when reduced for small-scale repeats. Tom Heron of Cresta Silks commissioned textile designs from Paul Nash, Cedric Morris, Bruce Turner, and his son Patrick Heron. Duncan Grant produced a number of designs for Allan Walton Textiles.

In 1953 The Institute of Contemporary Art in England staged an exhibition called Painting into Textiles. Twenty-five painters and sculptors—

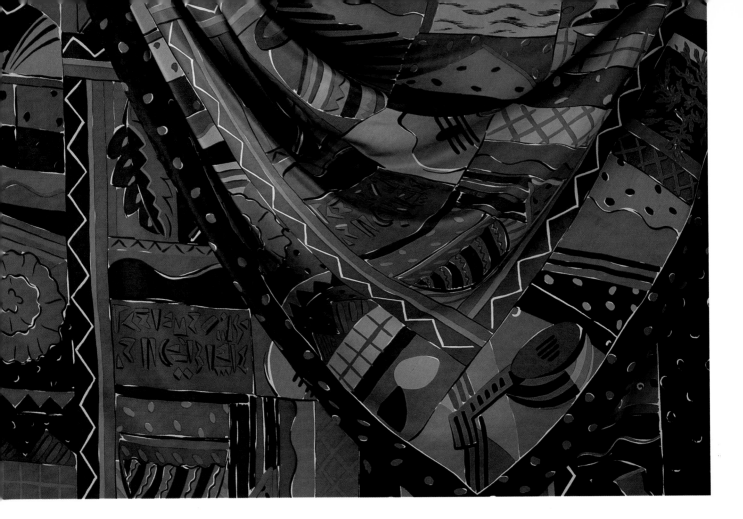

including Henry Moore, Ivon Hitchens, Eduardo Paolozzi, Victor Passmore and John Piper—were commissioned to produce paintings and drawings rather than designs so that they would not be inhibited by the restrictions of manufacturing techniques. By then, dyes were becoming more reliable and sophisticated, and screen printing had become fully mechanized, so cloth could be treated in a painterly way with good results. In the years after the exhibition many artists were invited to design for the most progressive manufacturers. Hans Tisdall created "Barges", a screen-printed cotton, for Edinburgh Weavers in 1956, and Elizabeth Frink designed "Warriors", a Jacquard-woven wool, for them in 1960. Eduardo Paolozzi's "Portobello" was a screen-printed cotton for Hull Traders in 1959.

Fine art and fabric design still go well together today. The British designer Susan Collier trained as a painter and has always produced painterly designs. She designed for Habitat and Liberty and in 1979 formed the design company Collier Campbell with her sister Sarah Campbell. All Collier Campbell fabrics, whether stylized, abstract, floral or based on ethnic textiles, begin as paintings, and many still retain the effect of brush strokes after printing. The fabrics are instantly recognizable for their strong, subtle and rich colour schemes.

Collier Campbell are known for their inventive fabrics, and their confident designs in rich colours have a distinctive "painterly" quality. "Guitar", shown here, is a versatile recent design which is being used on silk scarves and soft furnishings.

⟜ Screen-printed Designs ⟞

Hand screen printing was extensively explored in the 1930s and was an important means of employing artists' designs. For Warners, Marion Dorn's "Acorn and Oakleaf", used on the *Queen Mary* in 1935, was very typical of the simple, limited-colour designs of the 1930s. "Songster", a screen-printed linen by a Miss Martin in 1944, depicting doves in cages with olive branches on a dark ground, had the informal, sketchy drawing resulting from the period's increased understanding of the technique.

By the 1950s screen printing had become the favoured way to print textiles and wallpapers. It was less expensive than block printing or roller printing and by then it was clear that screens could duplicate the styles of other, more painstaking techniques and so encompassed a wide range of styles, including those more typical of blocks, rollers or lino cuts. Screens could handle large selvedge-to-selvedge designs, and these—together with the use of more colours—became much more common as the process was mechanized in the late 1950s. The enthusiasm and creative energy of these post-war years brought witty and energetic designs, mostly of a stylized nature.

⟶ Exploiting the Screen's Potential ⟶

Screen printing suited simple, sketchy textile patterns, such as stylized skeleton leaves or wild flowers, both of which were common. Typical designs featured stylized everyday objects, from sources as diverse as the Willy Hermann Studio in Berlin and Ruth Adler Schnee in America. Others were in the manner of an engraving, using architecture as a source of the design. Artists' designs also exploited the screens' capabilities; for example, Edward Bawden's "Olympus" of 1957 had large cable-pattern wreaths alternating with rows of strawberry leaves twining through a Greek key, all rendered with impasto-like texture, while his "Night and Day" of the same year exploited the potential of photo silk-screening to produce a slightly reduced version of Bawden's original. In 1955 Warners gained permission to print in England a selection of designs by Greeff, who were contracting their own screen-printed fabrics in America. They included "Frieze", a lively portrayal of stylized horses, using pigments in a gesso-like manner, in a style new to the firm. The designs were well-received and caused much comment.

During the 1960s there was a blooming of textiles in enormous, fiercely bright, highly stylized and childlike flower prints whose style, proportions and uninhibited colourways were unique to this period. Alexander Girard, the American architect and designer, designed screen-printed textiles with simplified, stylized doves, cherries, nuts, clouds and flowers for the premier office furniture company, Hermann Miller. These are typical of 1960s screen-printing style, with their strong purples, blues and greys.

As colours grew warmer and duller in the 1970s, they were reduced by the end of the decade to muted shades. New screen-printing technology (the galvano screen, with honeycomb-like holes) allowed these delicate shades to be used in washes resembling watercolours, adding to today's design vocabulary one more medium which screens can successfully duplicate.

CHAPTER SIX

FLORA AND FAUNA

"Remember that the most beautiful things in the world
are the most useless; peacocks and lilies, for instance."

JOHN RUSKIN, *The Stones of Venice*, 1853

Nature provides a never-ending source of shapes, patterns and colours for the artist, so it is hardly surprising that it features so heavily in patterned fabrics. Even in the most abstract or stylized of patterns it is often possible to detect flower or leaf forms, with every artist representing a growing plant in a different way. Flowers, foliage, animals, birds, shells and other natural forms have all been used in myriads of different combinations, and some crop up again and again because of their beauty and interest.

As with other types of pattern, motifs have often followed fashions and events of the time. For example, a series of roller-printed textiles was based on Audubon's book *Birds of America* around the time of its publication early in the nineteenth century, and bird prints remained fashionable for another decade. When Victorian missionaries and botanists brought orchids, palms and other hothouse plants back from the tropics, these too became sources for designs. After Japanese ports were opened to Western trade, in the mid-nineteenth century, Japanese designs were all the rage, in the form of chrysanthemums, poppies, flowering fruit trees, dragons, symmetrically paired birds and other exotic animals and plants. And, early in the twentieth

⌒

Nature, not surprisingly, has provided endless
inspiration for wallpapers and textiles of every
description. This wallpaper, of unknown
provenance, though it is possibly Chinese, was
produced c. 1840.

century, when cottage garden flowers were popular among gardeners, they appeared too in the chintzes of the day.

— The Origins of Chintz —

Chintz—a cotton fabric, frequently glazed, and usually featuring a floral pattern, often on a light-coloured ground—is generally thought of as quintessentially English. Yet, as with so many European designs, the origins of chintz can be traced to the East. The Indians were the first to master the skills of painting and printing patterns on to cotton and linen using dyes and pigments with mordants (see pages 63–4) to stop the colours from fading. These textiles, which were imported into Europe from the seventeenth century, were mainly hand-painted, but elements were hand-blocked. The colours were bright, uninhibited and joyful.

Consisting primarily of intricate overall floral forms, the patterning was both meticulous and aesthetically satisfying, and there was considerable variety in the designs produced. Unlike the early printed fabrics of Europe, which were usually an attempt to imitate the more expensive woven fabrics of the time, the Indian printed patterns were distinctly based on close observation of flora and fauna, the harmony of their forms and their adaptability to the printing process. Indian designers showed considerable inventiveness and skill in the planning of the design.

An example of an eighteenth-century chintz in the Victoria & Albert Museum portrays a wonderful meandering garden of flowers, with no two flowers alike, in green, red, blue and gold. Another has a wealth of inventive detail, including leaf forms in ogival shapes, within which are several flowers in blue, red and green on a white ground. Another uses tiny flowers to make up the paisley motif in an overall, non-repeating pattern, painted in bright blues, red and dark green on white. Each flower is lovingly drawn, with tiny painted leaves and petals creating a lace-like tracery of pattern over the fabric.

Such were the painted and printed calicoes imported into Europe by the East India Companies in the seventeenth and eighteenth centuries. In France they were known as *indiennes* or *chittes* and in England chints or chintz, from the Hindu word meaning "speckled". Initially, the cloths were not available in large pieces and therefore were used only for such purposes as table carpets or stool covers. Gradually, however, as the European market grew, the Indians began to cater for Western needs, and the calicoes were then used also as curtains, bed and wall hangings, bed covers and even clothing. As trade increased, the colours and patterns were modified to conform to a more restrained style suitable for Europeans. Patterns were sent out to India from Britain, France and Holland, affecting the size, composition and style.

The Indian bed covers known as palampores were imported extensively. Perfect examples of Indian patterning, they have provided inspiration for

OVERLEAF: Nineteenth-century chintz patterns abound in contemporary document prints and wallpaper borders, such as these from Design Archives, Designers Guild and Colefax & Fowler (details on page 179).

ABOVE: An Indian rumal or ceremonial cloth, showing typical nineteenth century colouring and detail. It was made in northern India, where echoes of such patterns remain in use for block-printed bed covers.

hundreds of textile and wallpaper designs. The palampore is printed from a series of small blocks skilfully arranged to cover the whole surface with a leafy design incorporating birds and animals and sometimes huntsmen. A typical colour scheme would have a good deal of black and red with touches of yellow and green on a pale ground. Other Indian ceremonial cloths with similar colouring and patterning, such as the rumal, were also imported.

⟿ Early European Chintzes ⟾

Chintz became an established part of the decorations of European homes, a welcome relief from the formal, single-colour woven damasks from Italy.

European workshops were soon set up to produce chintz. These, however, were printed rather than painted (though some hand-painting might be done; the technique was known as "pencilling", "pencil" being the Old English word for an artist's paintbrush). The actual designs altered, too, becoming more eclectic.

In the mid-seventeenth century, workshops in Marseilles produced the first European chintzes, which were the precursors of today's familiar Provençal prints (see page 128). Others soon followed. The finest chintzes of the time came from the Oberkampf factory at Jouy-en-Josas, near Versailles. Though better known for its pictorial *toiles de Jouy* (see page 174), it produced thousands of highly coloured floral designs based on Indian prints. Many of the floral patterns were taken from local plants.

London block printers began producing chintzes in the late seventeenth century, creating floral designs of considerable delicacy and freedom, with frequent use of vertical or waved stripes on light grounds. During the eighteenth century laws restricting the production of chintzes held the industry back, but by the 1770s normal production was restored. America imported its chintzes from England, but by the end of the eighteenth century, it was printing its own, particularly in the Philadelphia area, where English printers had set up businesses after emigrating to America.

During the eighteenth and nineteenth centuries, small prints were produced in Switzerland, France and England, many of which were reminiscent of Indian and Persian designs.

⌁ Chintzes of the Past Two Centuries ⌁

By the nineteenth century, English chintz was much bolder and more like the Indian cloths, and England had built up a reputation for quality. The period covering the first sixty years of the nineteenth century was the great age of chintz, characterized by prints of exceptional charm and originality.

Brightly coloured naturalistic flowers were popular designs well into the nineteenth century, though the influence of the reform movement at the end of the century made chintz less popular in England. America, however, experienced a great revival of interest in the fabric around the turn of the century.

In English neo-Georgian interiors of the early part of the twentieth century, small- to medium-scale chintzes in soft colours were popular. Featuring "eighteenth-century" motifs such as stripes, flower garlands and swags, small bouquets and ribbons, they were known as Manchester chintzes because this city in the north of England was a major centre for the roller printing of such textiles. In the 1920s and '30s, larger-scale floral chintzes in richer colours became fashionable.

By the 1950s chintz had fallen out of favour in England, though not in

"Palm Tree and Pheasant", from the G P & J Baker archive, was block printed in England in madder colours c. 1815. It has the "tea ground" which was common at this time—as well as the Western version of Oriental design. "Island" patterns like this, in which the motifs are not joined, were a feature of block-printed cottons early in the nineteenth century.

the United States, but the emergence of the "English country-house" look in the years after the war brought a resurgence of interest in chintz which has been sustained ever since.

⟿ Chintz Patterns ⟿

A considerable amount of copying of designs was common between the English and the French. French cottons were, in the main, more formal in design. Often they would feature stripes made up of floral motifs, or the floral motifs might be framed in a gold stem-and-foliage pattern. Cotton was sometimes printed in red only, in very delicate tiny designs. English chintzes often depicted English flowers, in such colours as blue, red and yellow, with leaves in green. The early ones were more realistic and less fantastic. But the variety was, and still is, enormous—from pretty florals joined by ribbons and bows, to florid large roses and passion flowers surrounded by buds, convolvulus and leaf posies. Often the flowers are quite European, featuring ivy, pea flowers and cornflowers, for example. Western design styles gave rise to all sorts of naturalistic forms, such as sprigs, garlands and bouquets.

One type of design popular from the early 1800s, and especially liked in America, was the "island" pattern, in which each motif is separated from its neighbours in repeat. Island patterns often had a tea-coloured ground and might outline the design with a narrow, undyed band. Such designs were also popular in Japan. They may have originated as block prints, as it was easier to print such patterns by hand blocking.

Chintzes have always maintained a degree of popularity, though they were more in fashion during some periods than others. Revivals of a particular style of chintz from an earlier period also occur. For example, manufacturers in the early nineteenth century produced adaptations of late eighteenth-century chintz designs with baskets of flowers, exotic birds and rococo scrolls. In the 1930s there was another late eighteenth-century revival, by designers like Frank Price of the Silver Studio, featuring urns, roses and twining foliage. Such designs are still popular today.

Wallpapers also use chintz designs in profusion. One paper from Temple Newsam (see page 73) illustrates the sort of progression a pattern could make. Dating from around the 1870s, it portrays cranes and storks as part of a striped pattern. It was taken from a French cotton print of a century before, which itself had probably been taken from an English cotton that possibly originated in an Oriental textile.

⌒ Modern Chintzes ⌒

Chintz has never lost its appeal. It has now become a generic term meaning "floral cotton" which is often glazed and encompasses a variety of styles, including the overblown rose. Many early-Victorian chintzes are reproduced on printed cottons today. The styles of chintzes are endless. They can be floral or geometric, large-scale or tiny, simple or exotic, lavish or subdued. American decorators have mastered the art of putting two or more chintzes of similar tonal values but different scales together to create a coordinated interior. The dictum of one of Britain's leading interior design companies, Colefax & Fowler, is that if you use chintz you should use a lot of it, though their hallmark has been to restrict this to one pattern throughout a room.

Screen printing technology lends itself to modern chintz design. The introduction in 1963 of nickel-coated mesh screens allowed subtleties of printing and is much used now for superior-quality prints.

Among the most successful and inventive producers of chintz today is Tricia Guild of Designers Guild in London. Her elegant range of chintzes (including designs by Kaffe Fassett and Howard Hodgkin) shows an individual sense of colour and pattern and an ability to produce overall designs of great style. Flowers are used in nearly all Designers Guild designs, and the coordinating collections are highly versatile. The screen-printed "Grandiflora" collection is an outstanding example of a large-scale floral design which does not dominate its environment. Tricia Guild's particular forte is in introducing so many patterns and colourways, any or all of which will look

The exotic flora on this Japanese sake bottle was widely copied on wallpapers and chintz prints, becoming ever more eccentric under western influence.

This amusing wallpaper panel is typical of early chinoiserie designs, which are now more rare than the original Chinese wallpapers they imitated. Produced in England around 1760, it depicts a fanciful, exotic view of the East, with all sorts of flowers springing from one shrub.

good together. She now uses discharge techniques and halftone screens to achieve an interesting depth in her floral designs.

In the United States, Brunschwig & Fils produce an enormous range of exquisite screen-printed cottons, such as "Westbury Bouquet", which features large flower heads and leaves on a dark ground.

Many of France's floral prints are still of the very highest standard. The French company Boussac produces marvellous screen-printed satin-weave cottons with fresh interpretations of ancient motifs, such as passion flowers, poppies, anonymous leaves and butterflies. Also in France, Manuel Canovas designs and produces some of the most creative and fresh floral prints available. He has recently started to use rayon/cotton mixtures in woven damasks in which the patterns are vigorously portrayed and simply coloured.

⌁ The Chinese Taste ⌁

Imported items from the Far East, such as Indian chintzes, Chinese silks, Chinese paper hangings, lacquerwork and porcelain, were popular in European aristocratic circles from the seventeenth century, and by the eighteenth century a passion for all things Eastern was ruling Europe. Out of this

emerged a new style of interior decoration based on pseudo-Oriental motifs, particularly exotic flora and fauna. Later called chinoiserie, "the Chinese taste" as it was known at the time was at its zenith in the 1740s and early 1750s but remained popular for bedrooms throughout most of the eighteenth century.

Like Gothick (see page 95), chinoiserie was a manifestation of the lighthearted and fanciful Rococo style prevailing in Europe at the time. It had less to do with the real China than with an imaginary, picturesque Cathay—a world of dragons, mandarins and pagodas. The Blue Willow patterned earthenware that first appeared in the 1760s typified this romanticized imagery.

Oriental motifs were emulated and often exaggerated on a variety of Western furnishings. Dining chairs had "pagoda-roof" cresting rails, and furniture was decorated with the angular fretwork known as "Chinese Chippendale". Carpets had pseudo-Chinese motifs, screens depicted "Oriental" scenes, and lacquerwork and japanning were used lavishly. Sometimes whole rooms were decorated in "the Chinese taste", but more often it was combined with Rococo, especially in intricate carving and plasterwork.

Chinoiserie designs showed an extraordinary mixing of East and West, with Indian, Chinese and Japanese influences intermingled. Twining leaves and plants might be copied from Chinese or Japanese lacquerware or porcelain. One tree might have several different types of flower growing from it—nothing was necessarily true to life. The fact that a design was exotic was often considered sufficient for it to pass as Chinese.

English and Continental manufacturers produced block-printed or hand-painted wallpapers in imitation of the expensive hand-painted Chinese wallpapers (see page 186). As with the genuine article, birds and flowers predominated, and squirrels, monkeys, fruit and other animal and plant life also featured. Some chinoiserie papers used cut-out figures and birds. Usually the Western character of these wallpapers is apparent, but a few bear a close resemblance to Chinese papers in terms of the actual artistry. Jean Baptiste Réveillon, the leading French paper-stainer of the eighteenth century, who was best known for his classical Pompeian designs (see pages 79 and 172), also produced wallpapers containing chinoiserie motifs such as exotic flowers or little pagodas.

Although chinoiserie faded from fashion towards the end of the eighteenth century, it experienced a major revival in Regency Britain. There was renewed interest at the end of the nineteenth century, when peacocks, dragons and phoenix were popular themes. Motifs associated with the Orient such as chrysanthemums, poppies and fruit trees in blossom were favourite designs of Arthur Silver, who founded the Silver Studio in 1880. Liberty of

Jean Baptiste Réveillon set an example of quality in manufacture and design which was almost unrivalled. As well as the Pompeian designs for which he is best known, he also produced chinoiserie patterns such as for this wallpaper and border, block printed c. 1789. The striking orangey-red colour appeared in most of his wallpapers.

London began printing silks with small floral designs that were exact reproductions of old Indian prints.

In the early years of the twentieth century, chinoiserie patterns appeared in a new guise, with brightly coloured, stylized motifs such as lanterns, fretwork and exotic birds and flowers printed on a dark ground. Popular in the neo-Georgian interiors that were the fashion then, these designs were considered too overwhelming for rooms other than halls and bedrooms.

Woven silk chinoiserie designs were also popular. A typical pattern was "Foo Chow", woven by Warners in 1927 and featuring islands of tree, leaf and flower forms with figures and birds.

Chinoiserie chintz patterns became fashionable too. The Silver Studio was turning out thousands of designs of flowering branches, tropical birds, cabbage roses and pagodas. They were wonderfully opulent in rich lacquer colour schemes such as red, black and gold, which blended perfectly into the Art Deco style of the 1920s and '30s (see pages 50 and 113).

⟶ The Japanese Style ⟵

Japanese-inspired birds, insects and flowers in brilliant colours were also a feature of many wallpapers and textiles manufactured in Britain and America in the late nineteenth century. By the 1890s the Japanese style had become

something of a craze. Exhibitions in both England and America had brought Japanese arts and crafts to the public's attention, and the re-opening of Japanese ports to trade with the West brought a flood of Japanese goods on to the market. The pervasive Japanese influence led to the development of the Aesthetic movement (see page 44). In 1875 Arthur Liberty, himself an enthusiast for the Japanese style, founded his London store, which became synonymous with the Aesthetic movement. It sold fabrics, furniture, carpets and bric-a-brac imported from the Far East and Near East and also specially commissioned textile designs, some of them Japanese-inspired. In America, Louis C Tiffany designed influential Aesthetic interiors.

Walter Crane's 1877 design for the dado paper "Swans and Rushes", block printed by Jeffrey & Company. The pattern was Japanese-inspired, and was for use with an "Iris and Kingfisher" wallpaper, also by Crane, and with an iris frieze.

Japanese furnishings used to a greater or lesser degree in most interiors of the time included blue and white porcelain, screens, peacock feathers, and bamboo or ebonized furniture. Hand-crafted Japanese artefacts such as fans, samurai swords, embroideries and lacquer boxes added to the overall effect of clutter.

The leading designer in the Japanese style was E W Godwin, who was much influenced by Japanese prints, which he collected. By the 1870s he was designing not only textiles but wallpaper in the Japanese style, with motifs such as fans and roundels known as "pies". Derived from the imported blue and white porcelain, these pie motifs were widely and indiscriminately used in Anglo-Japanese decoration of all kinds. In some silks of the period they appeared alongside Japanese-inspired birds, insects and blossoms, often in stylized small repeat patterns (see page 124). These textiles were frequently used with the ebonized furniture in fashion at the time. Other fabrics too used brilliant colours and Anglo-Japanese patterns such as exotic birds and flowers and Oriental emblems.

As well as Godwin, Japanese-influenced designers of the late nineteenth century included Owen Jones (whose "Nipon" design in silk tissue for Warners, for example, featured squares and octagons interspersed with stylized flower and leaf motifs with a distinctly Japanese flavour), Bruce Talbert, Walter Crane, G C Haite, Christopher Dresser, and Candace Wheeler. The Silver Studio produced many avant-garde Japanese-influenced wallpaper and textile patterns. A number of John Illingworth Kay's designs for them were based on Oriental landscapes, often with a strong vertical emphasis. Wallpapers were often printed in Japan from British designers' patterns. Alexander Rottmann's factory in Yokohama, for example, printed numerous Silver Studio designs.

The stylized, symmetrical shapes of paired birds that appeared in some of the textiles of the time and in Walter Crane's "Swans and Rushes" wallpaper were Japanese-inspired. This image was also incorporated into Art Nouveau (see page 129), which was itself influenced by Japanese art.

⌒ William Morris Floral Prints ⌒

Naturalistic flowers and fruit were characteristic of early Victorian textiles and wallpapers; initially, they were superimposed on Classical architectural backgrounds, but in the 1840s they were intertwined with elaborate scrolls and cartouches. By the 1850s, however, design innovators such as A W N Pugin and Owen Jones had rejected this naturalism in favour of flat, formalized patterns. John Ruskin, whose theories on design and architecture had an enormous effect during the second half of the nineteenth century, rejected the whole repertory of Renaissance-Classical decorative motifs (rosettes, fruits, etc.) as "prefabricated".

William Morris, the guiding light of the Arts and Crafts movement of the 1870s and '80s, generally shared the views of Pugin, Jones and Ruskin. He believed, however, that flowers used in textile and wallpaper designs should be seen to be growing naturally. Motifs from nature, though flattened and stylized, were clearly outlined and recognizable in his patterns. They retained their fundamental characteristics, yet their style was emphasized.

Morris and the other Arts and Crafts artists were drawn to the natural world for their imagery. Birds were popular subjects, appearing with fruit or among foliage. Morris himself eschewed the exotic hothouse plants so popular with the Victorians and instead drew his floral motifs from his own garden and the English countryside. Marigolds, honeysuckle, jasmine, lilies and eyebright were among the flowers depicted in his designs.

Morris believed that the structure of patterns was of crucial importance, as he explained: "... if the lines of them grow strongly and flow gracefully, I think they are decidedly helped by the structure not being elaborately concealed." His designs were rigorously constructed, on either a symmetrical diamond design framework or a branch framework that created a bower effect. Willow boughs or scrolling acanthus leaves were used as this structural background in a number of Morris's designs. Many of his designs also included complex, subsidiary patterns of small flowers growing from meandering stems. His insistence on the highest standards of design is apparent in this quotation:

> ... no amount of delicacy is too great in the drawing of the curves of a pattern, no amount of care in getting the leading lines right from the first. Remember that a pattern is either right or wrong. It cannot be forgiven for blundering. A failure forever recurring torments the eye.

Morris set up the firm of Morris, Marshall, Faulkner & Co in 1861. It began to sell printed fabrics in the late 1860s and woven fabrics in the early '70s. In 1875 "the Firm" (as Morris and his colleagues called it) was reorganized as Morris & Co; it continued trading until 1940, when it went into voluntary liquidation. Morris's patterns are still extremely popular today, among designers as well as the public, and screen-printed reproductions of some are available.

Whereas Morris's work of the 1860s and early '70s was characterized by free-flowing patterns, from 1876 until 1890 his designs have a more formal structure. During this period he designed a number of bold, imposing patterns with large repeats, for houses by the architect Philip Webb. From 1890 the patterns became less rigid again.

William Morris's increasing interest in historic images tended to make his later designs more complex. From 1876 to 1883, the most prolific period of his pattern designing, eleven wallpapers and twenty-two chintzes were

Rich with late Victorian naturalism, three William Morris fabrics—reproductions produced by Liberty (lower left) and Sanderson (lower right)—join forces with an Arts and Crafts reprint (top right), also by Liberty. The wallpaper is Morris from Liberty, and the Laura Ashley wallpaper borders are modern versions capturing the Arts and Crafts style.

produced. His chintzes became some of the best-known patterns ever to be produced. They were in marked contrast to the flowing, spontaneous, naturalistic designs of the early prints. This was partly the result of his work on the looms and also his intensive studies at the South Kensington Museum (now the Victoria & Albert Museum). A member of the museum's Acquisitions Committee, Morris was particularly influenced by English and French art of the Middle Ages and Italian fifteenth- and sixteenth-century woven fabrics. He revelled in Islamic and Persian textile designs, which he described as "fertile of imagination and lovely in drawing and colours". As he once said, "To us pattern designers, Persia had become a holy land, for there in the process of time, our art was perfected, there, above all places, it spread to cover for a while the world, east and west."

⌁ The Weaves and Wallpapers of William Morris ⌁

The most influential designer of the nineteenth century, Morris created designs not only for printed textiles but also for weaves, such as the damasks he designed for St James's Palace in 1866. He produced a number of designs for silk damasks, one brocatelle, several woven wool tapestries, and a limited number of silk-and-linen and silk-and-wool tapestries. Morris tried weaving velvet with gold tissue in the fifteenth-century Florentine manner and produced a blue, white and orange velvet pile with gold thread interwoven in parts. Only a small quantity was ever produced, however, because it was so expensive. He also designed a number of double-cloths (intended as wall hangings), embroideries (which were among the first textiles he produced) and hand-knotted carpets (he became an authority on Persian and Turkish carpets). With each, he immersed himself in all the techniques involved so that he could oversee every stage of production from start to finish.

It was William Morris who, more than anyone else, was responsible for wallpaper being regarded as a decorative art in its own right. An architect by training, Morris believed that wallpaper patterns should not attempt to create three-dimensional effects, since the function of the paper was to cover a flat surface. In a lecture Morris told his audience:

> I think the real way to deal successfully with designing for paper
> hangings is to accept their mechanical nature frankly, to avoid falling into
> the trap of trying to make your paper look as if it were painted by hand.
> Here is a place, if anywhere, for dots and lines and hatchings; mechanical
> enrichment is the first necessity in it. After that you may be as intricate
> and elaborate in your pattern as you please, nay the more and the more
> mysteriously you interweave your sprays and stems, the better for your
> purpose as the whole thing has to be pasted flat on a wall and the cost of
> all this intricacy will but come out of your own brain and hand.

"Fruit", one of William Morris's first three wallpaper designs, features pomegranates, peaches and lemons on a blue ground patterned with delicate tracery. Less symmetrical than his later designs, it was designed in 1862, produced in 1864 and reproduced by Sanderson in 1991 under the name "Pomegranate".

The colours Morris used for his papers, such as soft sage, rust and saxe blue, were more muted than his bright prints. Some papers were coordinated with cretonnes (printed furnishing fabrics coarsely woven from cotton and hemp, jute or linen).

⌁ The Arts and Crafts Movement ⌁

The Arts and Crafts movement took its name from the Arts and Crafts Exhibition Society, launched by Morris in 1888 after the Royal Academy refused to include the work of decorative artists in their exhibitions. Arts and Crafts artists, designers and craftsmen viewed the Middle Ages as the golden age of craftsmanship, forming themselves into medieval-style guilds. C F A Voysey was one of the movement's most influential members. An architect, Voysey designed every detail of his houses. Like Morris he created many designs, incorporating animals, hearts, flowers and trees, for wallpaper, prints, weaves and carpets.

Lindsay Butterfield, Arthur Silver, the architect Baillie Scott, Lewis F

Day, Heywood Sumner, and Walter Crane were other successful designers who produced Arts and Crafts designs.

The U.S. furniture style associated with the Arts and Crafts style was known as "craftsman" or "mission" style. Morris's ideas were influential in America, where Associated Artists (founded in 1879 by Louis C Tiffany, Candace Wheeler, Samuel Colman and Lockwood de Forest) followed the basic principles of the Arts and Crafts movement. In particular, the colours used in their interiors were close to those used by the British movement. Candace Wheeler herself designed embroideries, textiles and wallpapers, winning Fuller & Company's 1881 wallpaper design competition. Her designs were mainly floral, with a strong Japanese flavour, overlaid detail and tone-on-tone effects. Associated Artists was dissolved in 1883, but Candace Wheeler continued to design textiles for over twenty years more, and a number of smaller societies were formed in America at around that time, dedicated to the same simplicity in design, traditional design sources and practical products.

⌒ Floral Patterns ⌒

Flowers and foliage have played a more important part in textile and wallpaper design than any other design source, particularly in the patterning of printed fabrics. Today there is a passion for flowers in design, whether taken from document fabrics and papers, or completely new motifs.

The acanthus has been widely used since early times. A plant with boldly indented and scrolled leaves, it was a common element in Greek and Roman architectural ornament and a widely used Renaissance motif. It has appeared on textiles and wallpapers over and over again, from Italian velvets to Arts and Crafts prints. William Morris said of it, "No form of ornament has gone so far or lasted so long as this; it has been infinitely varied, used by almost all following styles [ie after the Greek] in one shape or another, and performed many another office besides its original one." Large leaf *verdure* tapestries, employing foliage in soft greens, tans and browns on a dark blue ground, were manufactured in France and Flanders in the sixteenth century, and greatly influenced William Morris's tapestries. Many designs of the 1890s, including a number of William Morris prints, incorporated the large, swirling patterns of acanthus scrolls or other classical floral motifs from sixteenth- and seventeenth-century Italian woven silks, other European textiles and hangings, and English embroidery.

The "Acanthus" wallpaper design by William Morris, with its grand sweep of foliage, was so elaborate that it required a double set of blocks and 32 printings. It was first produced in a red colourway, then in combinations of greens (as seen here) and of yellowish-browns.

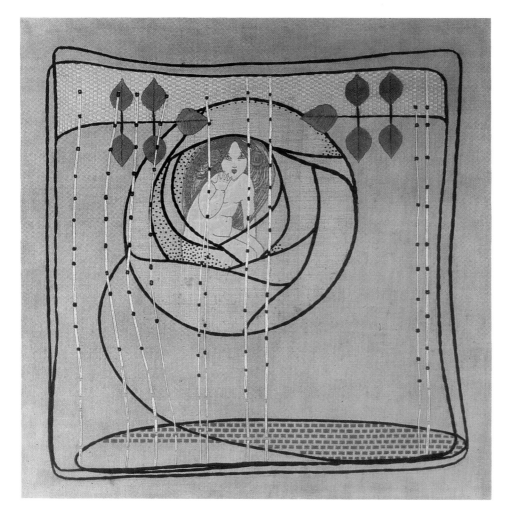

LEFT: Charles Rennie Mackintosh, his friend H J McNair, McNair's wife Frances and Frances's sister Margaret Macdonald worked together, developing a common style. The similarity of "The Spirit of the Rose", designed and embroidered by Frances McNair c. 1900, to Mackintosh's stylized rose (shown opposite) is apparent.

OVERLEAF: Flowers and foliage have provided a rich source of inspiration for wallpapers and printed textiles, and their common theme makes possible joyous combinations of an infinite variety of patterns.

Charles Rennie Mackintosh's spare little Art Nouveau cabinet incorporates the stylized rose associated so strongly with his fabric print designs.

The rose is as beloved in textile and wallpaper design as it is in the garden, because of its colour, robust shape and different forms, ranging from tiny rosebuds to full-blown cabbage roses. It became a standard motif for Victorian chintz. Rosebuds would be used for dainty fabrics and wallpapers intended for ladies' boudoirs and for servants' or children's bedrooms. A brightly coloured all-over design of roses and leaves roller-printed by Maquiestor & Company in America was typical of American chintz patterns of the Victorian period, receiving an award for "premium damask" from the American Institute in 1850. In the twentieth century, the English interior design company Colefax & Fowler's "Rosa Mundi" chintz reflected its co-founder John Fowler's love of striped roses, and "Old Rose" is one of their most successful prints.

In the last quarter of the nineteenth century, block prints nearly always used natural motifs and were often based on the exotic plants which were brought back by botanists from all parts of the world. Such flowers as rhododendrons, lilies, poppies and chrysanthemums were often connected by trailing vines or ribbons. The Victorians relished dense, all-over floral designs featuring huge roses mixed up with lilacs and other flowers, in spite of criticism from the Arts and Crafts movement that the popular three-dimensional effects and florid realism were inappropriate for flat walls.

Certain garden plants became popular for use with specific styles. The rose featured in Art Nouveau designs by Charles Rennie Mackintosh and the Glasgow School (see page 133). Its trailing stems and thorns fitted the style well, though as an Art Nouveau motif it became very stylized, lost all its individual petals and became more of a pompom. Other plants useful to Art Nouveau style because of their long, shapely leaves or stems were lilies, irises, tulips, poppies and bulrushes.

Nasturtiums, with their curious, almost geometric leaves and bright orange colour, were widely used in Art Deco textiles and pottery. Pansies too suited the Art Deco style, for their shape and colour.

⁓ Modern Florals ⁓

American textile designer and producer Jack Lenor Larsen specializes in using power looms and man-made fibres with ethnic resist-dyeing techniques (see pages 103–107) for luxurious and very beautiful fabrics for the mass market, including airlines and contract furnishing companies. Jason Pollen for the Larsen Design Studio created a spectacularly beautiful fabric with a pattern of freesias in blues, purples and reds on a midnight ground.

Inger Elliot of the American China Seas Fabric House imports batik-dyed cloths from Java (see page 105). Palms and exotic flowers, with a finely dotted background, feature in these centuries-old patterns, which were

ABOVE: Stylized roses were often used by Charles Rennie Mackintosh, as in this design for a printed textile.

RIGHT: Although Jack Lenor Larsen is best-known for his abstract designs, he has also produced some highly individual floral patterns, such as this Jacquard weave, "Anastasia".

influenced by the China trade and the Dutch colonists. These very intricate patterns are produced in rather brighter colours for the West than the traditional indigo, brown and white of Java.

Scalamandré, of the United States, produces very fine tapestry weaves using several sets of coloured warps and several wefts to achieve an extraordinarily subtle shading effect, in which whole jungles can be created with exotic flowers, tall trees, and large and small leaves. England's Osborne & Little have many ranges of floral fabrics and wallpapers, such as "Peony Pots", a glazed cotton screen-print with a bold repeat pattern of Chinese porcelain pots holding peonies. The Japanese designer Kazumi Yoshida's "Papiers Japonais" in cotton percale consists of very delicate, almost botanical drawings of flowers and leaves arranged as separate sheets on an antique brown ground.

In the 1960s and '70s the depiction of plants became almost photographic in its meticulous drawing. Many designs were taken from photographs or watercolours for highly naturalistic, extremely detailed floral designs of both wild flowers and garden plants. Gloriously exotic designs by Althea McNish, the Trinidadian designer based in England, depicted flowers seen in the Caribbean or on her travels.

Foliage patterns without flowers are popular too. Some take their inspiration from carved glass, as in the monochrome screen-print "Normandie" produced by the American firm Clarence House.

⌐ Animal and Bird Designs ⌐

Second only to flowers and foliage, birds and animals have featured in almost every kind of wallpaper and textile, particularly prints. Peacocks, partridges, herons, birds of paradise, pheasants, cocks and doves have all had their place.

The peacock, in particular, has appeared in many guises. Edward Godwin's emblematic design "Peacock" was inspired by his sketches of Japanese embroidered badges; he used it in single repeat as a frieze or in double repeat as a dado. The peacock could be combined with a choice of fillings and borders based on Oriental motifs. Arthur Silver enjoyed using the peacock motif, and he made it the basis of "Hera", a design for Liberty in 1888 which became their trademark. Louis C Tiffany used the colours of peacock tail feathers for his glassware. A frieze by W Dennington, manufactured by Shand Kydd Ltd in 1900, was a colour block print of a peacock; the bird is superimposed on a stylized arrangement of climbing roses, rather restrained in style and resembling a stained glass window. The prolific designer Walter Crane, who produced fifty wallpaper designs for Jeffrey & Company from 1874, included peacocks in some of his designs.

Other birds and animals have also featured again and again. Birds were employed in the seventeenth century to enliven and fill the spaces left empty

Whether designing for Cavendish Textiles (John Lewis Partnership) or the English National Trust, since the 1960s Pat Albeck has been noted for her stylized floral designs such as this lively black-and-white print.

This delicately drawn wallpaper, dating from 1840, is possibly of Chinese origin. Certainly it is typical of the meticulous observation of nature and skilled work found in Chinese wallpaper. The cuckoo, kingfisher, butterfly and peony are all accurately drawn, unlike most European imitations produced at around the same time.

between the bunches of flowers or twining plants used in the decoration of the period. Aubusson tapestries (see page 184) portrayed turkeys and birds of paradise. The Chinese and Japanese included cockatoos, carp and butterflies in their designs—not to mention dragons.

Many William Morris designs included birds. The first wallpaper he designed (the third in production) was "Trellis", with intertwining roses and brown birds perched among the branches. Morris diffidently refrained from designing the birds himself and got his friend and partner Philip Webb to do them for him. "I am studying birds now to see if I can't get some of them into my next design," he wrote—the result was the famous "Bird", a treble-woven cloth in a much more controlled and sophisticated design than his prints had been. "Flora," designed around 1885 by Edward Burne-Jones and Morris, is a wool-and-silk tapestry on a linen warp, with pheasants, rabbits and partridge in the design.

CHAPTER SEVEN

PICTORIAL DESIGNS

"... Whatever is of Art or Nature, may be introduced
into this Design of fitting up and furnishing Rooms with
all the Truth of Drawing, Light and Shadow and Great
Perfection of Colouring."

JOHN BAPTIST JACKSON, *An Essay on the Invention of Engraving
and Printing in Chiaro Oscuro*, 1754.

Pictorial designs are those which are figurative rather than stylized or
abstract. Finely detailed and beautifully drawn, they generally depict
a complete scene or an artefact such as a coin. Pictorial designs often
look as though they have been taken from painted, engraved or sculpted
originals. They may involve *trompe l'oeil* effects (deceiving the eye with such
devices as false perspective in order to suggest than an image is real).
Architectural elements such as columns, pilasters, pediments and arches and
Classical images such as urns, plinths and busts are frequently used. Because
of their strong pictorial quality, these designs are intended to be seen flat,
rather than draped or folded, so fabrics are usually used as panels, cushion
covers or upholstery. Wallpapers are obviously an ideal medium, and, in fact,
over the years pictorial designs have been dominated by the wallpaper
manufacturers, who have produced some remarkable images.

⟶ Early Pictorial Papers ⟵

During the sixteenth and seventeenth centuries, a number of pictorial papers
depicting outdoor scenes and religious or mythological subjects, possibly
inspired by tapestries, were block printed in black-and-white and sometimes

⟶

With the renewed interest in Neoclassicism, *toiles de
Jouy* have enjoyed a revival since the late 1980s. The
red and purple draped fabrics shown here are
antique French toiles; the blue is new from Laura
Ashley. The framed fabrics are reproductions from
The Design Archives, and the wallpaper is from
Cole & Son (details on page 195).

hand-coloured afterwards. They were used as lining papers or occasionally as wallpapers in the wealthiest homes. Chinese elements were sometimes incorporated.

The leading French paper-stainer of the early eighteenth century, Jean Papillon, produced large pictorial scenes that might fill an entire wall. The outlines of these designs were block printed, then the colouring—either watercolour or ink—was added with brush and stencil.

⁓ Pompeian Designs ⁓

From around 1770 until 1789, another French firm, Réveillon (see also page 79), produced complex Neoclassical wallpapers widely regarded as the most artistic ever created. They featured Classical arabesques (fanciful vertical patterns combining foliage, fruit, vases, animals and figures) which imitated Pompeian paintings, particularly for use in decorative panels. Only the wealthy were able to have their walls hand-painted in the Classical manner, but wallpapers made this style of decoration available to many more customers.

Réveillon employed a number of designers, including the Italian artist Cietti, who was skilled in imitations of stucco and Pompeian marble. Jean Baptiste Fay and Lavallée-Poussin were two other artists specializing in imitations of Pompeian paintings. Some of Réveillon's most popular patterns were copied in textiles.

When his factory was burned by a mob at the beginning of the French Revolution, Réveillon and his wife escaped to England. The business was sold to Jacquemart et Bénard, who continued to produce Pompeian designs, often indistinguishable from those of Réveillon himself, until Republican themes (such as tricolour ribbons) overtook them.

Although only two Réveillon wallpapers have been found in England, the papers were imported at the time. However, Pompeian designs were never as popular in England as they were in France.

⁓ Chiaroscuro Block Prints ⁓

During the mid-eighteenth century, colourful, elaborate pictorial papers were produced by John Baptist Jackson (see also page 76), the only English paper-stainer of the period about whom much is known. In fact, at one time nearly all examples of this type of paper were attributed to Jackson. In his colour printing he used only oil colours, a medium which subsequently fell into disuse, but the techniques he developed in his papers completely altered the wall decoration of the period. Inspired by the chiaroscuro engravers of the Italian Renaissance, Jackson perfected his chiaroscuro technique of multi-coloured block printing to create three-dimensional effects in imitation of painting, sculpture and architectural details.

John Baptist Réveillon often used classical arabesques such as this in his wallpapers. This Réveillon wallpaper panel was hand-painted c. 1780–1790.

In *An Essay on the Invention of Engraving and Printing in Chiaro Oscuro*, published in 1754, Jackson explained the value of his printing techniques:

> ... the Person who cannot purchase the Statues themselves, may have these Prints in their Place; and may effectually shew his Taste and Admiration of the ancient Artists ... Or if Landscapes are more agreeable, for Variety Sake Prints done in this manner, taken from the Works of Salvator Rosa, Claude Lorrain, Gaspar Poussin, Burgher, Wavermann, or any other great Master in the Way of Painting, may be introduced into Pannels of the Paper, and show the Taste of the Owner ... No Figure is too large for this Invention, Statues and other Objects may be taken off in full length, or any size whatever.

The style pioneered by Jackson of using wallpaper to imitate large architectural designs was very fashionable for the decoration of halls and staircases of grand houses during the second half of the eighteenth century, when Neoclassical decoration (see page 35) was the vogue. *Trompe l'oeil* ceiling papers imitating plasterwork and stucco work, borders simulating architectural cornices and ornaments, and wallpapers imitating oak panelling with columns and alcoves were all used a great deal—sometimes replacing the real thing. Wallpapers decorated with imitations of gilt-framed landscape paintings and still-lifes were popular too.

Block printed papers simulating Gothic tracery were fashionable as part of the Gothic style popularized by Horace Walpole (see page 95), who used

Wallpaper featuring this sort of *trompe l'oeil* tracery was a fashionable part of the Gothic Revivals of the late eighteenth and mid-nineteenth centuries. Looking like the carved stonework of medieval church windows, such papers were considered suitable for staircases and passages.

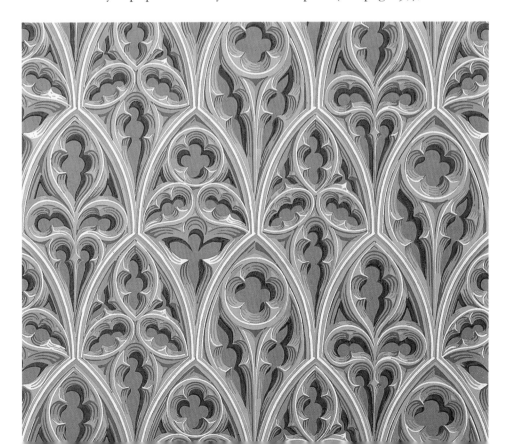

Jackson's "Venetian" prints in the decoration of Strawberry Hill. The papers were frequently pasted on to staircase walls. Other Gothic papers imitating medieval architecture, screens and trellis were also used, employing shadows and perspective so as to look like carved woodwork or the carved stonework around church windows.

⌒ Toiles de Jouy ⌒

At the height of the eighteenth-century fashion for Neoclassical wallpapers, the printed cotton fabrics known as *toiles de Jouy* flourished. Printed from engraved copper plates (see page 65) in single colours on an off-white ground, these prints featured finely detailed pictorial scenes resembling the Neoclassical wallpapers of the time and were used as flat wall panels. The finely etched lines created a rich variety of tonal effects, giving the fabrics great charm and interest.

Typical designs included rustic scenes of everyday life, pastoral landscapes, ancient buildings, Classical figures and motifs, chinoiserie fantasies, events of the time (such as the first balloon flight and the end of the American War of Independence) and mythological subjects. The prints contained the most minute detail, be it ripples in the water, distant birds wheeling in the sky or a woodland grove with a group of people leading horses.

By the end of the eighteenth century, some prints had pictorial designs within bordered panels, on a ground pattern of repeat motifs such as lozenges, rosettes, circles or small medallions, making them look very like framed prints hung on a papered wall.

Toiles de Jouy were usually printed in blue, violet, red or sepia using vegetable dyes, particularly madder, indigo and woad. Occasionally extra colours were added by block printing the fabric as well. Prior to printing, the cloth—which initially was imported from India but subsequently was manufactured *in situ* at the factory's own mill—was repeatedly washed and bleached and afterwards was calendered (passed through rollers) to produce the soft "toile".

The name *toiles de Jouy* derived from the Oberkampf factory at Jouy-en-Josas, near Versailles, which produced a large number of these copperplate-printed calicoes, of a very high standard, from 1770. (The Oberkampf factory had been block printing multicoloured floral designs since 1760 but became better known for their monochrome "toiles".) Copperplate printing of cottons had been done in Ireland from 1752 and in England from 1757, and English "toiles" of a similar style developed along parallel lines. Nevertheless, it was the imported French cloths that latterly were the best known. Oberkampf was a perfectionist, insisting on the highest standards of design, using the best-quality materials, and employing the most talented artists and skilled workers.

RIGHT: Patriotic images depicting George Washington, Benjamin Franklin, Liberty, and the thirteen states of the new American republic feature in this copperplate-printed "toile" produced in Britain c. 1785 for the American market. It was printed in at least three colourways (blue, red and purple).

OVERLEAF: *Trompe l'oeil* is an intriguing feature of much pictorial design. The British design company Timney Fowler have made their mark with monochrome printed textiles and wallpapers, such as the designs shown here (details on page 195).

Toiles de Jouy, now a generic term for this type of print, are produced at a number of factories. They are often used today in the traditional French manner: in abundance all over a room.

⌒ Nineteenth- and Twentieth-century Neoclassicism ⌒

Neoclassical designs of the nineteenth century became increasingly heavy and oppressive, in both England and France. In the first half of the century, wallpapers imitating draped silk and other fabrics with tassels, fringes and cords were produced by such firms as Jacquemart et Bénard. Some were very subtle, others quite colourful and crude. Their three-dimensional, *trompe l'oeil* appearance was condemned by critics as being "quite absurd" copies of something that was already rather overdone in the first place. At around the same time, wallpaper friezes imitating stucco work and sculpture were very popular in France.

Towards the end of the century firms such as Lightbown, Aspinall & Company produced wallpapers that emulated hand-ornamented distemper ceilings, with a central rose and imitation-plaster flowers in geometric shapes.

Today, a number of designers, in particular the English design company Timney Fowler, are producing architectural prints by using black on a white background, with fine lines and detailing. Their Classical architectural motifs include arches and columns, pedestals and wrought iron. Timney Fowler's bestselling design "Emperors' Heads" has an enormous pattern repeat:

104 cm/42 inches. Other typical designs include "Urns and Drapes", "Columns" and "Small Roman Heads". Very striking because of their sense of scale, their monochromatic simplicity and the power of the designs, these prints combine tradition with a strong contemporary feeling.

⌐⌐ The Art of Tapestry ⌐⌐

Whereas architectural prints and wallpapers are based on engravings and sculpture, tapestries are taken primarily from paintings. For much of their history, the style of tapestries produced at a particular time followed the style of paintings of the period. Indeed, the narrative quality of the design, the fine, detailed workmanship and the wealth of colour are factors contributing to their fascination and splendour. Yet the increasingly slavish imitation of paintings that occurred between the sixteenth and nineteenth centuries was also to lead to tapestries' near demise, as they began no longer to be seen as art forms in their own right.

Basically, a tapestry is a hand-woven decorative fabric in which the design is built up during the weaving process. (Sometimes the term is also used for machine-woven textiles—see page 18.) Hand-woven tapestry is different from most other forms of patterned weaving in that the weft threads are not carried the full width of the fabric; each is only woven in where that colour appears in the design. Tapestries have traditionally been used in the West primarily as wall hangings, which allows their narrative quality to be appreciated fully.

The material most commonly used for European tapestries has always been wool, but many have combined a wool warp with a linen, silk or cotton weft, which adds variety and textural contrast and is more suitable for fine detail. Silk can be used for highlights and to add a luminous sheen; it was particularly common in European tapestries of the eighteenth century, when it was used to create subtle tonal effects. Gold and silver weft threads have sometimes been used along with wool and silk for a sumptuous effect.

Many themes have been represented in tapestries, particularly stories from the Bible and fables, battle scenes, great historical events, hunting scenes, incidents from everyday life and scenes of chivalry and courtly love.

Ever since the Middle Ages, tapestries have been woven from artists' designs known as cartoons, which the weaver would embellish or refine. The medieval cartoon was painted on a canvas the same size as the tapestry to be woven and might be re-used for other tapestries a number of times, with adaptations as necessary. (The client's coat of arms, for instance, might be incorporated in a border, and other details might be altered to update the scene.) The tapestry was very much a joint creation of artist and weaver. In the sixteenth century Raphael prepared a set of cartoons depicting the "Acts of the Apostles", and the following century Rubens produced a set called the

A selection of antique tapestries: (Clockwise from top) eighteenth-century tapestry screen, (on table) seventeenth-century tapestry panel, (bottom left) pair of eighteenth-century *verdure* cushions, (on chair) eighteenth-century tapestry and silk velvet cushions, and (at left, behind chair) eighteenth-century tapestry.

"Triumph of the Eucharist". Both sets were re-used and imitated many times. Today, tapestry cartoons may be produced from photographic enlargements of the model (the original source of the design) or numbered diagrammatic drawings.

⌐ Flemish Tapestries ⌐

European tapestry flourished from the beginning of the Gothic period (see page 94) in the thirteenth century. By the fourteenth century, when it was introduced into England, it was well established in Europe. Paris and Flanders, particularly the city of Arras, were the two greatest centres of the industry; in fact, "arras" became a generic term meaning tapestry. The famous "Angers Apocalypse" dates from this period. Produced in Paris in around 1377, it consisted of seven tapestries, each 5 metres/16 feet in height and 24.4 metres/80 feet in length.

European tapestry weaving reached its peak in the fifteenth century, when the greatest tapestries were produced in the Flemish cities of Tournai, Brussels and, initially, Arras. The designs of these Gothic tapestries were closely related to painting styles of the time, but they did not try to *look* like paintings. "The Hunts of the Dukes of Devonshire", a set of four tapestries now at the Victoria & Albert Museum in London, is regarded as very typical of the type of work produced by the Tournai weavers of the mid-fifteenth century. Many of the Tournai tapestries were vast and monumental, incorporating heavy outlining.

During the Middle Ages, tapestries were extensively used in the grandest and wealthiest homes, adding comfort and colour to otherwise spartan rooms. Because medieval households moved around a great deal, tapestries were transported from house to house. (The twentieth-century architect Le Corbusier described them as "nomadic murals".) Although they were frequently woven to fit a particular room, more often than not they did not fit exactly and would consequently be cut up to fit the dimensions of new rooms as necessary. Tapestries extending over doorways or around corners were commonplace.

Hangings would be ordered by the "chamber"—a chamber being all the textiles needed for the walls of a room along with bed hangings and coverlets, and cushions and seat coverings. Although they were often designed as single panels, tapestries were also frequently produced as sets, with perhaps six or more panels in the set.

By the mid-fifteenth century Brussels had become known for its "alterpiece" tapestries. Reproducing Flemish religious paintings, such as "The Adoration of the Magi", they were produced for use in churches or chapels and were therefore much smaller than the tapestries of Arras and Tournai. Silk was often used in them to obtain the required detail. In the late fifteenth

and early sixteenth centuries, Brussels was known for its profusion of golden threads in such works as "The Glorification of Christ".

At this time the tapestries known as *millefleurs* were also being produced in Brussels and Bruges and by itinerant Flemish weavers in France, particularly the Loire valley. These consisted of flora and fauna on a red or dark-blue ground, which served as a background to heraldic devices or scenes of medieval chivalry.

By the sixteenth century, war and persecution had forced many Flemish weavers to become refugees, and they followed the example of nomadic Flemish weavers of the previous century in setting up tapestry workshops around Europe, from England to Italy. Brussels had become the leading tapestry centre of Flanders, remaining so until the seventeenth century. Other Flemish tapestry centres in the sixteenth century were Enghien and Oudenaarde (both producing *verdure*, or garden, tapestries) and Grammont, Alost, Lille and Tournai.

Having reached its zenith during the Renaissance, tapestry weaving began

This arabesque tapestry designed by Joshua Morris in 1720 was woven in London's Soho Workshop. It incorporates many of the most traditional textile motifs, such as the large urn, acanthus leaves, tulips and large garden roses.

gradually to decline, as the weaver became the artist's imitator rather than his collaborator, and tapestries became more like copies than original works of art. By the end of the fifteenth century the weaver was probably working, not from a cartoon, but from the model, such as a painting. Increasingly fine threads were being used in order to create more naturalistic detail, a process which continued over the next three and a half centuries. (Whereas the fourteenth-century "Angers Apocalypse" had about 5 threads per cm/12 per inch, some tapestries of the nineteenth century had as many as 16 threads per cm/40 per inch.)

It was during the Renaissance that decorative borders in imitation of picture frames began to be incorporated in tapestries, many of them featuring contemporary strapwork motifs.

⌒ English Tapestries ⌒

England was importing vast quantities of tapestries by this time. Henry VIII had well over 2,000 and was said to employ a small army of tapestry makers and menders.

All walls that were not panelled were covered with textile hangings. Households no longer moved frequently around the country, so tapestries tended to be more permanent too. In a few instances, rooms were actually built to accommodate existing tapestries.

In the 1560s William Sheldon set up the first important English tapestry manufactory in Warwickshire. The Sheldon works continued into the seventeenth century, producing some works of high quality, in particular a series of large maps of English counties, taken from engravings.

The Sheldon works was, however, overshadowed by another English factory, at Mortlake, near London, founded in 1619 under the patronage of James I. Before its decline in the 1680s, the factory produced a number of tapestries for the court of Charles I and wealthy patrons. Towards the end of the seventeenth century, other small tapestry works were set up, the most important of which was the Soho Workshop. Many of the Soho tapestries were designed by John Vandebank, including some chinoiserie hangings for Kensington Palace.

⌒ French Tapestries ⌒

In 1538 Francis I established a factory at Fontainebleau, near Paris, to make tapestries for his royal residences. Woven by Flemish weavers from cartoons by two Italian Mannerist artists, the tapestries included a series of six based on a mural at Fontainebleau; they were the first examples of tapestries using *trompe l'oeil* effects to imitate sculpture as well as painting. This workshop was active for only twelve years, but it led to the development in the mid-sixteenth century of a Paris tapestry factory.

A mid-eighteenth century tapestry depicting Saturn, woven at the Gobelins works near Paris. The factory at this time was specializing in *alentours* tapestries like this, with ornamental motifs surrounding a "framed" central subject.

In 1601 France prohibited the importation of tapestries, to protect the French weaving industry. This gave a considerable boost to the small industry at Aubusson, where Flemish weavers had set up workshops. They began producing a wide variety of hangings, upholstery fabrics and carpets of a high quality, in particular chinoiseries, *verdures* and architectural panels. In 1665 the Aubusson works was granted royal patronage.

In the same decade, the Gobelins tapestry works near Paris (making tapestries since 1529) was established as a royal manufactory, and a factory established in 1664 at Beauvais was given royal patronage. In the late seventeenth century, decorative panels produced at Beauvais depicted complex architectural scenes, as well as "grotesques"—architectural tracery framing motifs such as festoons, vases, masks and musical instruments. Their "Fables of La Fontaine", by Oudry, were among the most popular of all eighteenth-century tapestries. Some of the best-known tapestries produced at Gobelins were the eighteenth-century *alentours*, in which elaborate ornamental motifs surrounded a central subject made to look like a painting framed in gilded wood. The *alentours* tapestries "Loves of the Gods" were particularly popular with the English nobility.

Textiles were still in fashion for grand rooms in eighteenth-century English houses, and designers such as Robert Adam successfully designed rooms around Gobelins tapestries. However, flock wallpapers (see page 75) and carved panelling had replaced tapestries on many walls. (As an interesting footnote, in around 1750 French flock wallpapers were produced which imitated not velvets and damasks like the English flock papers, but tapestries. To produce them, paints mixed with adhesive were applied by hand, and the flock in the appropriate colour was scattered on to the paint before it had dried. The finished papers closely resembled real tapestries—but the adhesives did not resist damp, and as a result there are no surviving examples of this ingenious technique.) Another nail in the coffin of tapestry weaving, already declining in fashion in France, was the French Revolution. As an art form, tapestries had always been associated with privilege and luxury, and many beautiful old tapestries were consequently destroyed during the Revolution. Machine-made tapestry, introduced in the nineteenth century, was a further threat.

⟵ Regeneration of the Craft ⟶

Towards the end of the nineteenth century, William Morris and the English Arts and Crafts movement (see pages 46 and 158) turned back to the ideals of medieval craftsmanship, and breathed new life into the art of tapestry weaving. Morris—who when watching a patriotic, tourist-oriented tapestry being woven at the Royal Windsor Manufactory (opened in 1876) had thought, "It would be a mild word to say that what they make is worthless ... It is more than that. It is corrupting and a deadening influence upon all the lesser arts of France"—was motivated five years later to set up a tapestry factory at Merton Abbey in Surrey. The Pre-Raphaelite painter Sir Edward Burne-Jones produced most of the designs, although Morris and the illustrator Walter Crane also designed a few cartoon sketches. (Morris had himself learned to weave, and his first tapestry, "Vine and Acanthus", took him over 500 hours to make in 1879.)

The architect A H Mackmurdo (see page 133) produced a number of adventurous designs in the 1880s, and many other artist-craftsmen also followed Morris's lead. At about the same time in Europe, there was a revival of tapestry weaving based on folk art.

In the twentieth century, tapestry attracted the interest of modern artists. Many allowed their paintings to be reproduced as tapestries by the Aubusson factory in 1932. Such great artists as the painter Henri Matisse and the architect Le Corbusier have designed representational tapestries, and the painters Georges Braque, Jean Arp and Victor Vasarely have produced abstract designs. In 1962 Graham Sutherland designed "Christ in Glory", which was woven at Aubusson, for Coventry Cathedral in England. One of

the most ambitious tapestries of the century, it measures 23.8 × 11.6 metres/
78 foot 1 inch × 38 foot 1 inch and is the largest tapestry ever woven at
Aubusson.

The real breakthrough, however, was made by the French artist Jean
Lurçat in the 1930s. Influenced by Gothic tapestry and especially "Angers
Apocalypse", Lurçat—in collaboration with François Tabard, master
weaver at Aubusson—formulated the principles that made tapestry again an
art form in its own right. As a result, the coarse textures and bold but limited
range of colours of the Middle Ages once more characterize tapestries.
Today, the art of tapestry weaving is flourishing in centres such as the
Edinburgh Tapestry Company, also known as the Dovecot Studios.

⌒⌒ China Papers ⌒⌒

Colourful, hand-painted pictorial wallpapers from the East were the height
of fashion in the homes of wealthy Europeans from about 1740 to 1790.
Imported from China by the East India Companies from the late seventeenth
century until well into the nineteenth century, these "China papers" were
sometimes inaccurately called "India papers" or even "Japan papers". It is
likely that they were based on the painted silk hangings found in the homes
of wealthy Chinese but were actually produced specifically for export, as
there is little evidence of wallpaper being used in Chinese homes at that time.

The papers were hand-painted in brilliant colours by artists who were at
pains to capture every detail as it really was. Even the butterflies were
representative of known species. The majority were painted on a single-
coloured background (most often green, blue or tobacco brown) and
depicted plant and animal life, such as birds and insects, shrubs and flowering
trees. Trees in full blossom would climb the height of the paper, with birds
perching and butterflies and insects flying around. Sometimes there might
be details like a rocky pool, a low ornamental balustrade, clumps of bamboo,
potted shrubs or lanterns in the foreground, and birdcages would occasionally be shown hanging from branches. Other papers showed hunting scenes
or everyday life in China, sometimes combined with plant and animal motifs.

Cantonese merchants exported the papers in sets of 25–40 rolls, each roll
made up of several sheets pasted together and bearing a number to indicate in
what order the rolls should be hung. Spare rolls were often supplied so that
extra motifs, such as birds or branches, could be cut out and pasted on. The
papers contained no repeating patterns, and so could create a continuous
panorama around a room, though the designs had no depth and made no
attempt to disguise the two-dimensional nature of the wall. Often walls were
not hung with the complete panorama but instead were covered with a series
of individual scenes separated and framed by strips of plain paper.

The wallpapers were relatively expensive, particularly as they came in sets.

A Chinese wallpaper from the second half of the eighteenth century, depicting the ever-popular hunting scene. Other themes incorporated plant and animal motifs.

Thomas Chippendale recorded that among his purchases for Sir Rowland Winn, there were thirty-six sheets of Chinese papers, since "the person they belong to will not sell them separate, nor will he take under 15s a sheet".

⟶ The Indian Market ⟵

Interestingly, in the late nineteenth century a few British manufacturers developed pictorial papers for the Eastern market. Panels showing Indian gods, for example, were produced for religious festivals; one of the papers in the "Hindoo Gods" series by Allan Cockshut & Company showed a boating party with a lambrequin overhead from which hung Oriental lanterns; fish were swimming beneath, and the men wore pagoda-like turbans. Such papers were highly coloured and quite unrealistic, not to say brash.

⌐ French Scenic Papers ⌐

Shortly after hand-painted Chinese wallpapers went out of fashion at the end of the eighteenth century, there appeared another type of wallpaper—known as scenic paper— which was similar in concept to the Chinese papers, and perhaps partially inspired by them. Depicting Classical stories and architecture, exotic lands and luxuriant flora and fauna, scenic papers quickly became popular in France, where they were produced, and in America, though they made less impact on the English market.

Like the Chinese papers, the French scenic papers were designed to be placed in sequence on all four walls of a room, to form a continuous panorama. (Often however, they were cut up and used in panels "framed" by strips of paper.) The earliest examples did actually repeat at intervals around the room, but by 1804 the first scenic paper without a repeat— Jean Zuber's "Vues de Suisse"—had appeared.

Some of the panoramas were enormous; one of the largest measured 16 metres/52 feet long and 3 metres/10 feet high. Generally, they were fixed on to a canvas backing and hung so as to clear the floor by 1.2–1.5 metres/ 4–5 feet, so that the design could be viewed fully without furniture getting in the way.

Although the first scenic papers were hand-painted, wallpaper manufacturers soon rose to the challenge and began block printing them. They were printed on panels made up of small sheets of paper stuck together to form longer lengths. From 1830, with the introduction of continuous paper, they were produced in rolls. Designing and printing scenic papers was time-consuming and expensive. The designs showing the distribution of the printing blocks had to be enlarged to full size. Even for the grisaille designs (those printed in shades of grey), several hundred blocks, each measuring about 45 × 50 cm/18 × 20 inches, were often needed, and in some designs over two hundred colours were used. The printing worked to an exact order, with darker shades and broader areas done first, and lighter tones and details filled in later. Each layer had to dry before the remaining colours could go on, so a complete set might take up to two years to complete. In spite of this, an astonishing number of designs was produced during the first half of the nineteenth century.

⌐ Panoramic Subject Matter ⌐

City architecture was a popular subject for scenic papers. "Monuments de Paris", for example, which was produced in 1814 by Joseph Dufour (whose company became Dufour et Leroy in 1820) after designs by Jean

The scenic paper "New York Bay" was produced by Zuber in 1861 for the US market. The overall width of these panels is 3.29 metres/10 feet 10 inches. The panels would have been hung so the joins were not apparent.

Broc, was a panorama of the chief buildings of Paris. They were arranged elegantly along the Seine, with strolling sightseers and grazing cattle dotted picturesquely along the river bank. As in other topographical papers by Dufour, such as "Vues de Londres" and "Vues d'Italie", considerable artistic licence was allowed in the design. (One of the possible sources of inspiration for "Monuments de Paris" was another fad of the time, a painted panorama displayed on a cylindrical surface, which bore the same title. Like other novelty "panoramas" of this type, it was exhibited in a specially constructed rotunda in a Paris park.)

Other papers by Dufour depicted mythological subjects. His 1816 illustration of the Cupid and Psyche legend, designed by Louis Lafitte and Mery-Joseph Blondel, was made up of twenty-six panels arranged in twelve separate scenes, printed in shades of sepia or grisaille. The set required 1,500 wood blocks to print it. It may have been based on a painting by Pierre Joseph Proudhon, "Psyche Carried Off by the Zephyrs". Dufour also produced a "Lady of the Lake" and a "Cid" panorama.

Another endlessly popular theme was that of exotic lands. Dufour's "Les Sauvages de la Mer Pacifique", one of his earliest papers, was composed of twenty rolls of paper and depicted the adventures of Captain Cook. Dufour's "Vues de l'Inde" included Indian landscapes and temples.

There were also a number of other manufacturers of scenic papers. Jean Zuber's firm prospered throughout the nineteenth century, but after his non-repeating "Vues de Suisse" appeared in 1804, he waited two decades before producing another scenic paper, "Paysage des Lointains". One of his most interesting scenic papers, depicting different types of horse-racing in France, England and Italy, was "Courses des Chevaux".

Exotic garden scenes were a speciality of the firm Desfossé et Karth, who became associates in 1865 and continued to produce papers until after the Second World War. Their "Décor Eden" took well over three thousand blocks to print. It featured a peacock, lyre bird and parrot, surrounded by cockatoos, hummingbirds, butterflies and other flying creatures, with a misty blue forest and palm trees in the background. Zuber's landscape "Eldorado" was similar in feeling.

Emile Delicourt had worked with Dufour before establishing his own company (taken over by Desfossé in mid-century) and was another leading manufacturer of scenic papers. "La Grande Chasse", his most famous decoration, received the highest award at London's Great Exhibition of 1851. His wallpaper "Africa" (also known as "Cleopatra") was produced for a series called "Five Parts of the World"; it was made up of five panels, each representing a continent.

Because of the great popularity of the scenic papers in the United States, designs specifically for the American market were created by the French manufacturers. From the 1830s Zuber produced papers depicting Niagara Falls, Boston and other American scenes, as well as one commemorating the War of Independence. "New York Bay" was a panoramic wallpaper produced by Zuber in 1861.

American factories were soon set up to manufacture scenic wallpapers. M H Birge & Company, who set up their factory in Buffalo, New York, in 1834, specialized in complex panel decorations and ornament based on the Gothic mural paintings of Notre Dame Cathedral in Paris.

As well as full-sized wallpapers, a large number of scenic friezes were produced in France in the first half of the nineteenth century. Similar in

A single panel from the scenic paper "Les Monuments du Paris", block printed in 1814 by Joseph Dufour. City architecture was a popular subject for scenic papers, though considerable artistic licence was taken.

concept to the full-sized papers, they depicted continuous scenes which would run around the upper portion of the walls of a room.

⌒ Nursery Papers ⌒

Although pictorial wallpapers were produced from the eighteenth century, nursery papers only appeared in Victorian times. Fragments of a cylinder-printed pattern of the 1840s found in London show Mr Punch and other well-known comic characters and scenery of the time.

Commemorative papers were popular for Victorian nurseries. Brightly coloured and "educational", they celebrated events ranging from Wellington's victories and Queen Victoria's Golden Jubilee (complete with vignettes of her colonies), to Derby Day and the London Boat Race. Wallpapers depicting sport, such as "Bicycling", produced by Higginbottam, Smith in Manchester, were another popular subject for children's rooms.

Many nursery papers of the time presented an idealized vision of childhood, such as little girls and boys playing in well-kept cottage gardens, wearing the inevitable sunbonnets, and riding in homemade carts pulled by the faithful family dog. Nursery rhymes—such as a "Bo-peep and Simple Simon" frieze by Will Owen, produced in 1910 by Lightbown, Aspinall & Company—were also popular subjects.

Walter Crane, one of the most famous of all children's book illustrators, designed many children's wallpapers and friezes (see page 83) in the late nineteenth century. Kate Greenaway was another successful illustrator who also designed nursery papers, and her light, open designs, depicting beautifully dressed little boys, and dainty girls in sunbonnets, were highly popular.

Nursery friezes were popular from late-Victorian times until the 1930s. Seaside scenes were favourite subjects, since the advent of the railways enabled people to visit the seaside for day trips or holidays.

Some of the best nursery papers, such as this Liberty design of the 1930s, have a timeless quality that makes them as charming now as they were when they were first produced.

Like a number of other nursery papers, her series "The Months" was washable. Kate Greenaway inspired many papers of the "innocent childhood" genre, and in fact a number of anonymous papers exist illustrating nursery rhymes and legends in this style.

Other illustrators who turned their hand to nursery papers included Randolph Caldecott, with his lively, amusing illustrations of nursery rhymes; Mabel Lucy Attwell, whose round-eyed children were considered very sweet; and Cecil Aldin, who was well-known for his animals, especially dogs. A frieze based on Beatrix Potter's inimitable illustrations for *Peter Rabbit* has been in continuous production since it first appeared; since the mid-1980s it has been produced by Prelude Designs of the United States.

American children's wallpapers were similar, if a little less prissy. "Montauk", with its matching frieze, depicted children with slightly more cartoon-like faces, though they were enjoying the same sort of activities, such as skipping rope, playing with dolls and tobogganing.

After the First World War, Walt Disney's Mickey and Minnie Mouse became popular for children's rooms, and Sanderson produced a Mickey

The cheerful nursery wallpaper and fabrics of Designers Guild's "Abracadabra" collection, released in 1991, have much in common with children's art.

Mouse border around 1930. Typical of 1950s screen-printed nursery papers is Christina Risley's "Joanna" for the "Palladio" range by Wallpaper Manufacturers Ltd. Taken from a pen-and-ink drawing, it depicts doll-like children, toys and animals, with each motif "framed" in leaves. Sections of Shand Kydd's "Focus" series of pattern books of the 1960s were devoted to nursery designs, including well-known storybook favourites such as Paddington Bear. Crown Wall Coverings produced papers covered in soldiers, airplanes, vintage cars, spacemen and The Flintstones cartoon characters.

The history of textiles spans thousands of years and hundreds of civilizations, and, together with wallpaper patterns, takes in an almost infinite number of designs, providing endless inspiration for the homes of today. Of course, ultimately the choice of wallpapers and textiles depends on personal taste, and, once again, one of William Morris's dictums goes to the heart of the matter: "Have nothing in your home which you do not know to be useful or believe to be beautiful."

ACKNOWLEDGEMENTS

~

My thanks to the many people who helped with this book, including Liberty for giving permission to use their fabric for the cover; Mary Schoeser, for her invaluable contribution; Tim and Zoë Hill, for their splendid photography; Lynda Marshall, for her inspired and painstaking picture research; Harry Green, for his intelligent, stylish design; Gillian Haslam for her continual support and encouragement; and the many people who helped with information and transparencies, especially:

The Colour Museum, Bradford

Lesley Hoskins of Sanderson Archive

Dorothy Bosomworth of Warner Archive

Maud Wallace and Christine Woods of the
    Whitworth Art Gallery

The London Library

The Victoria and Albert Museum Textiles
    and Prints Departments

Pat Albeck

Aste Textile Co

Backhausen

Brunschwig & Fils

Colefax & Fowler

Nick Colwill of Colwill & Waud

Belinda Coote

Tricia Guild of Designers Guild

Althea McNish

Les Olivades

Felicity Osborne of Osborne & Little

Simon Playle

Eddie Pond

Mary Poole

Eddie Squires

Bernard Thorp

Philippa Watkins

Toni Willis

And special thanks to Alison Wormleighton, my editor.

PICTURE ACKNOWLEDGEMENTS

Patricia Albeck p 168; American Museum in Britain pp 39, 96–7; G P & J Baker p 151; Bridgeman Art Library pp 26, 94, 124, 133, 152, 164 bottom/Belvoir Castle, Rutland pp 74–5/Château de Malmaison p 27/Colnaghi & Co p 20/Fine Arts Society p 164/ Grimsthorpe Castle p 182/Musée Cluny p 181/private collection pp 24, 88/Rose Castle, Cumbria pp 144, 169/Victoria & Albert Museum pp 22, 23, 35, 47, 49, 65, 78, 99, 125, 127, 129, 147, 156, 161, 162–3, 165 top, 172, 184; Colefax & Fowler p 80; Collier Campbell p 142; Belinda Coote pp 18–19; Crown Wall Coverings p 135; Designers Guild p 193; Joss Graham pp 102, 104–5, 106; Tim Hill pp 2–3, 8, 11, 14, 17, 42–3, 51, 57, 58, 61, 62, 70–1, 84–5, 92–3, 100–1, 108–9, 119, 130–1, 132, 148–9, 159, 166–7, 170, 176–7, 179, 191; Kinnasand pp 5, 30–1, 55, 208; Jack Lenor Larsen pp 29, 120, 165 bottom; Liberty of London Prints, cover and endpapers, pp 32, 44–5, 48, 64, 64–5, 134, 140, 192; Marimekko p 117; Althea McNish pp 1, 52–3; Philadelphia Museum of Art p 175; Arthur Sanderson & Sons pp 72–3, 81, 112–13, 138, 139; Schwartz-Huguenin p 13; Jim Thompson Silks p 121; Victoria & Albert Museum by courtesy of the Board of Trustees pp 21, 25, 36, 40–1, 66, 67, 69, 76–7, 83, 86–7, 91, 110–11, 122, 153, 173, 187, 190; Warner Fabrics pp 6, 60, 115; Watts & Company p 95; Whitworth Art Gallery pp 82, 116, 136, 154–5; Zuber & Cie pp 188–9.

DETAILS OF ROOM SETS

pp 2–3: Antique shawls, THE ANTIQUE TEXTILE COMPANY, 100 Portland Road, London W11 4LQ. "Grand Paisley" printed fabric, WARNER FABRICS, 7–11 Noel Street, London W1V 4AL.
p 8: "Eye Dazzler" rug, TWINLIGHT TRAIL, 2 Buckingham Lodge, 2 Muswell Hill, London N10 3TG. Large rug and Navajo artefacts, THE AMERICAN WORLD OF COSTUMES AND PROPS, 6 Hainault Close, Hadleigh, Essex.
p 11: 19th-century striped silk damask (centre) and ecclesiastical brocade (bottom right), GALLERY OF ANTIQUE COSTUME AND

TEXTILES, 2 Church Street, London NW8 8ED. Modern damasks and brocades (clockwise from top left): French brocade, JOEL & SONS FABRICS, 77 Church Street, London NW8 8EU; linen and cotton varese and yellow damask, PIERRE FREY, 253 Fulham Road, London SW3 6HY; "Busby" damask, SIMON PLAYLE, 6 Fulham Park Studios, Fulham Park Road, London SW6 4LW; gold damask-patterned wallpaper, COLE & SON, 18 Mortimer Street, London W1A 4BU; green damask-patterned wallpaper from ARTHUR SANDERSON & SONS, 53 Berners Street, London W1P 3AD; tassels from SMITH & BRIGHTY, 184 Walton Street, London SW3 2JL.
p 14: Modern striped cotton Indian ikat, NICE IRMA'S, 46 Goodge Street, London W1P 1FJ. Modern Far Eastern cotton ikat, NEAL STREET EAST, 5 Neal Street, London WC2H 9PU. Persian, Indonesian, Philippine and central Asian ikats, Borneo baskets, African surveyor's staff, Sumatran spear, JOSS GRAHAM, 10 Eccleston Street, London SW1 9LT.
p 17: Ginghams, IAN MANKIN, 109 Regents Park Road, London NW1 8UR.
pp 42–3: Victorian curtains (top left, top centre, bottom right, bottom left), red/blue tile, blue glass storage jars with red/gold lids, tassels, JUDY GREENWOOD ANTIQUES, 657 Fulham Road, London SW6 5PY. Red/gold fabric (top right), LAURA ASHLEY, Braywick House, Braywick Road, Maidenhead, Berks SL6 1DW. "Mikado" chintz (centre right), damask-patterned flock wallpaper and red/gold wallpaper, COLE & SON, address as above. "Foliage" fabric (bottom centre) and "Bangalore" fabric (centre), MARVIC TEXTILES, 12–14 Mortimer Street, London W1N 7RD. Red/maroon wallpaper (in tin), ARTHUR SANDERSON & SONS, address as above.
p 51: "Sullivan" fabric from the Chiltern Collection, LIBERTY & COMPANY, address as above. 1930s pottery and coffee table, BEVERLEY, 30 Church Street, London NW8 8DT.
p 57: Vegetable dyes (clockwise from top right): marigold, lichen, alkanet root, lichen, stick lac, camomile, logwood chips, madder root, turmeric, broom, saffron, mollusc shells, cork oak bark, onion skins, GILL DALBY, "Clovers", Church Street, Alcombe,

Minehead, Somerset TA24 6BL. Reproduction medieval fabric dyed with madder and indigo (centre), woven by Craftsman's Mark for English Heritage, and Dornix 17th-century reproduction woven fabric, GILL DALBY, address as above. Other fabrics (clockwise from top left): Indian kalim kari bedspread, tablecloth and silk scarf, Bangladeshi block-printed silk scarf, Chinese tie-dye purses, Japanese kasuri fabrics (with raffia), Chinese tie-dye blouse, Japanese batik, NEAL STREET EAST, address as above.

p 58: Pink, peach, striped and plaid silk taffetas, OSBORNE & LITTLE, 304–308 Kings Road, London SW3 5UH. Orange taffeta (top right), ZIMMER & ROHDE, 103 Cleveland Street, London W1P 5PL. Two purple taffetas, LIBERTY & COMPANY, Regent Street, London W1R 6AH.

p 61: Wallpapers (top left, bottom right and background), JOHN OLIVER, 33 Pembridge Road, London W11 3HG. Two wallpapers (centre right) and borders, OSBORNE & LITTLE, address as above. Gold 19th-century brocade, red 19th-century silk woven with gold, and antique Chinese silk satin brocade, THE ANTIQUE TEXTILE COMPANY, 100 Portland Road, London W11 4LQ. "Palazzo" brocade (bottom left), ZIMMER & ROHDE, address as above.

p 62: Ashtrays, PENTAGRAM. Fabrics and other props, IKEA.

pp 70–1: Printed cottons, pillowcases, cushion covers, china, tray and antique linen, PUTNAM'S COLLECTIONS, 55 Regents Park Road, London NW1 8XD.

pp 84–5: 1920s fabrics, Archives of ARTHUR SANDERSON & SONS, 100 Acres, Oxford Road, Uxbridge, Middx UB8 1HY.

pp 92–3: Silk damasks and antique Gothic wallcovering, vestment and candelabra, WATTS & COMPANY, 7 Tufton Street, London SW1P 3QE. Parquet flooring, THE LONDON ARCHITECTURAL SALVAGE COMPANY, Mark Street, London EC2 4ER.

pp 100–1: Kilims, sofa, stool, box and cushions, DAPHNE GRAHAM, 1 Elystan Street, Chelsea Green, London SW3 3NT. Wallpaper and borders from "Sundance" range, HILL & KNOWLES, 358a Richmond Road, East Twickenham, Middx TW1 2DU.

pp 108–9: Antique tartan shawl, traditional rugs, antique silk wrap, modern tartan fabrics and pottery, ANTA, Fearn, Tain, Ross and Cromarty, Scotland IV20 1TL and 141 Portland Road, London W11 4LR.

p 119: Fabrics, screen, Lois Walpole baskets, Gerard Pigot parrot table and Stephanie Bergoman vases, COLLIER CAMPBELL, Downers Cottages, 63 Old Town, London SW4 0JQ.

pp 130–1: Fabrics: mauve on white "Coucareu" and black/gold "Bonis" (both on clothesline), blue "Maïanenco" and red "Pieta" (both far right), check "Escoussé" and green "Calendau" (both in basket), LES OLIVADES, 16 Filmer Road, London SW6 7BW. Red "Farandole" fabric and blue "Les Pompadours" fabric (both behind dolly), napkins (on clothesline), scarf, borders and hangers, SOULEIADO, 171 Fulham Road, London SW3 6JW.

p 132: "Astrid" wallpaper and "Atheneum" border, COLE & SON, address as above. "Hera" woven fabric, LIBERTY & COMPANY, address as above. 1920s silk velvet shawl, GALLERY OF ANTIQUE COSTUME AND TEXTILES, address as above.

pp 148–9: Wallpaper borders and chintz document prints: "Tapisserie" (top left), "Wild Rose" (top right), "Fiorita" (bottom right) and "Tapestry Flower" (centre left), DESIGNERS GUILD, 271 and 277 Kings Road, London SW3 5EN; "Sissinghurst" (top centre), COLEFAX & FOWLER, 110 Fulham Road, London SW3 6RL; "Victorian Ribbon" (centre right) and "Langport" (bottom left), THE DESIGN ARCHIVES, 79 Walton Street, London SW3 2HP.

p 159: Morris reproduction fabric (bottom right), ARTHUR SANDERSON & SONS, address as above. Morris reproduction wallpaper and fabrics: "Strawberry Thief" (bottom left) and "Melbury" (bottom right), and Art Nouveau reproduction fabric "Clementina" (top right), LIBERTY & COMPANY, address as above. Wallpaper borders, LAURA ASHLEY, address as above.

pp 166–7: wallpaper, ARTHUR SANDERSON & SONS, address as above. 3 large hat boxes (on settle), 2 rectangular boxes (under settle), THE EMPTY BOX COMPANY, The Old Dairy, Coomb Farm Buildings, Balchins Lane, Westcott, Nr Dorking, Surrey RH4 3LE. 3 hat boxes (on floor), 2 "rose" boxes (on floor and on settle), tin and old boxes (on settle), PUTNAM'S COLLECTIONS, address as above. Hat, gloves, shoes, GALLERY OF ANTIQUE COSTUME AND TEXTILES, address as above.

p 170: Red toile, French, 1785, by J B Huet, "Les Plaisirs des Quatres Saisons" and purple toile, French, 1810, "Le Temps Fait Passer l'Amour", THE ANTIQUE TEXTILE COMPANY, address as above. Blue modern toile, LAURA ASHLEY, address as above. Framed toiles: brown "Liaison" and green "Liaison", THE DESIGN ARCHIVES, address as above. "Classic Toile" wallpaper, COLE & SONS, address as above.

pp 176–7: Scarves, "Columns" wallpaper, "Angel and Pillar" cotton print curtains, "Sphinx" and "Statues" wallpaper borders, "Head" cotton cushion covers, "Statues" and "Gothic" velvet cushion covers, and "Head" plate, TIMNEY FOWLER, 388 Kings Road, London SW3 5UZ.

p 179: Chair, tapestry panels, screen, curtains, cushions, LINDA GUMB, 9 Camden Passage, London N1 8EA.

pp 191: Edwardian-style nursery frieze, rag rug, LAURA ASHLEY, address as above. Victorian and Edwardian toys, ALIVIN ROSS, Stand G009, Alfie's Antique Market, 13–25 Church Street, London NW8 8DT.

DIRECTORY

MUSEUMS AND ARCHIVES

The American Museum, Claverton Manor, Bath BA2 7BD, England. (Textiles and wallpapers)

The Cooper–Hewitt Museum, Smithsonian Institution, 2 East 91st Street, New York, NY 10028, USA. (Wallpapers)

Deutsches Textilmuseum, Andreasmarkt 8, 4150 Krefeld, 12-Linn, Germany. (Textiles)

Hôtel de Cluny, rue du Sommerard, Paris 5, France. (Tapestry)

Manchester City Art Gallery, Mosley Street, Manchester M2 3JL, England. (Wallpapers)

Manufacture des Gobelins, 42 Avenue des Gobelins, Paris 13, France. (Tapestry workshop, with tours)

Metropolitan Museum of Art, 82nd Street and Fifth Avenue, New York, NY 10028, USA. (Textiles and wallpapers)

William Morris Gallery, Lloyd Park, Forest Road, London E17 4PP, England. (Textiles and wallpapers)

Musée des Arts Décoratifs, 107 rue de Rivoli, Paris 13, France. (Textiles and wallpapers)

Musée de l'Impression sur Étoffes, 3 rue des Bonnes-gens, 68100 Mulhouse, France. (Textiles)

Musée du Papier Peint, 28 rue Zuber, 68170 Rixheim, Mulhouse, France. (Wallpapers)

Museum of American Textile History, 800 Massachusetts Avenue, North Andover, Mass. 01845, USA. (Textiles)

Museum of Art, Benjamin Franklin Parkway, Philadelphia, Pennsylvania 19101, USA. (Textiles)

Museum of Art, Rhode Island School of Design, 224 Benefit Street, Providence, RI 02903, USA. (Textiles and wallpapers)

Museum of Mankind (British Museum Department of Ethnography), 6 Burlington Gardens, London W1X 2EX, England. (Textiles)

Arthur Sanderson & Sons, 100 Acres, Oxford Rd, Uxbridge, Middx UB8 1HY, England. (Textiles and wallpapers)

Scalamandré Museum of Textiles, 201 East 58th Street, New York, NY 10022, USA. (Textiles)

Silver Studio, Middlesex Polytechnic, Bounds Green Road, London N11 2NQ, England. (Textiles and wallpapers)

Society for the Preservation of New England Antiquities, 144 Cambridge Street, Boston, Mass. 02114, USA. (Textiles and wallpapers)

Temple Newsam House, Leeds LS15 0AE, England. (Wallpapers)

Textil Museum, Domplatz, 8600 Bamburg, Bayern, Germany. (Textiles)

University of Washington Textile Study Center, Seattle, Washington 98105, USA. (Textiles)

Victoria & Albert Museum, Exhibition Road, London SW7 2RL, England. (Textiles and wallpapers)

Warner Fabrics, Tilbrook, Milton Keynes MK7 8BE, England. (Textiles)

Washington Textile Museum, 2320 South Street, Washington DC 20008, USA. (Textiles)

Whitworth Art Gallery and Museum, University of Manchester, Oxford Road, Manchester M15 6ER, England. (Textiles and wallpapers)

MANUFACTURERS AND SUPPLIERS

Louise Allrich Gallery (Textile Art), 251 Post Street, San Francisco, CA 94108, USA.

The Antique Textile Company, 100 Portland Road, London W11 4LQ, England.

Roger Arlington, 979 Third Ave, New York, NY 10022, USA.

Artek, Keskuskatu 3 PL 468, 00101 Helsinki, Finland.

Laura Ashley, 150 Bath Road, Maidenhead, Berks SL6 4YS, England and 714 Madison Ave, New York, NY 10021, USA.

Aste, Ulmerstrasse 121, PO Box 1152, D-7332 Eislingen, Germany.

Backhausen, A-1010 Vienna, Kaärntner Strasse 33, Austria.

Baker-Parkertex, 18 Berners Street, London W1P 4JA, England and through Lee Jofa, 800 Central Boulevard, Carlftodt, New Jersey 07072, USA.

Baumann, 4901, Langenthal, Switzerland and through Carnegie, 110 North Center Avenue, Rockville Center, NY 11570, USA and through Baumann-Kendix, 41–42 Berners Street, London W1P 3AA, England.

Boras Watveri, PO Box 52, S-50102 Boras, Sweden.

Boussac of France, 27 rue du Mail, Paris 75002, France and 979 Third Avenue, New York, NY 10022, USA.

Brunschwig & Fils, 979 Third Avenue, New York, NY 10022, USA and Chelsea Harbour Drive, London SW10 0XF, England.

Manuel Canovas, 7 place Furstenberg, 75006 Paris, France and 2 North Terrace, Brompton Road, London SW3 2BA, England and 979 Third Ave, New York, NY 10022, USA.

Carnegie, 110 North Center Avenue, Rockville Center, New York 11570, USA.

China Seas, 979 Third Avenue, New York, New York 10022, USA.

Clarence House, 211 East 58th Street, New York, NY 10022, USA and through Elizabeth Eaton, 30 Elizabeth Street, London SW1W 9RB, England.

Cole & Son, 18 Mortimer Street, London W1A 4BU, England and through Clarence House, 211 East 58th Street, New York, NY 10022, USA.

Colefax & Fowler, 39 Brook Street, London W1Y 2JE, England and through Cowtan & Tout, 979 Third Avenue, New York, NY 10022, USA.

Collier Campbell, 45 Conduit Street, London W1R 9FB, England and through Roger Arlington, 979 Third Avenue, New York, NY 10022, USA.

Belinda Coote, 29 Holland St, London W8 4NA, England.

Cowtan & Tout, 979 Third Ave, New York, NY 10022, USA.

Crown Wall Coverings, Belgrave Mills, Belgrave Road, Darwen, Lancs BB3 2RR, England.

The Design Archives, 79 Walton Street, London SW3 2HP, England and through Cowtan & Tout, 979 Third Avenue, New York, NY 10022, USA.

Designers Guild, 271 and 277 Kings Road, London SW3 5EN, England and through Osborne & Little, 65 Commerce Road, Stamford, CT 06902, USA.

Elizabeth Eaton, 30 Elizabeth Street, London SW1W 9RB, England.

Kaffe Fassett, 62 Fordwich Road, London NW2 3TH, England and through Ehrman, 5 North Boulevard, Amherst, New Hampshire 03031, USA.

Christian Fischbacher Co, Vadinstrasse 6, CH-9001, St Gallen, Switzerland and 913 Fulham Road, London SW6 5HU, England and through Stroheim & Romann, 31–11 Thomson Avenue, Long Island City, NY 11101, USA.

Anna French, 343 Kings Road, London SW3 6HY, England and through Classic Revivals, 6th floor, Suite 545, 1 Design Center Place, Boston, Mass 02210, USA and through Lee Jofa, 800 Central Boulevard, Carltfodt, NJ 07072, USA.

Pierre Frey, 47 rue des Petits-champs, 75001 Paris, France and 253 Fulham Road, London SW3 6HY, England and through Brunschwig & Fils, 979 Third Avenue, New York, NY 10022, USA.

Gainsborough Silk Weaving Company, Alexandra Road, Chilton, Sudbury, Suffolk CO10 6XH, England.

Galacar & Company, 144 Main St, Essex, MA 10929, USA.

Gallery of Antique Costumes and Textiles, 2 Church Street, Marylebone, London NW8 8ED, England.

Joss Graham, 10 Eccleston St, London SW1 9LT, England.

Christopher Hyland, Suite 1714, 979 Third Avenue, New York, NY 10022, USA.

Jamasque, The Glasshouse, 11–12 Lettice Street, London SW6 4EH, England.

Java Cotton Company, 52 Lonsdale Road, London W11, England.

Kinnasand AB, Box 256, S-51101 Kinna, Sweden.

Jack Lenor Larsen, 41 East 11th Street, New York, NY 1003-4685, USA and through ZR Clifton Textiles, 103 Cleveland Street, London W1P 5PL, England.

Lee Jofa, 800 Central Boulevard, Carltfodt, New Jersey 07072, USA.

Liberty & Company, Regent Street, London W1R 6AH, England and Rockefeller Center, Fifth Avenue, New York, NY 10022, USA.

Ian Mankin, 109 Regent's Park Road, London NW1 8UR, England and through Agnes Bourne, 550 15th Street, San Francisco, CA 94103, USA.

The Manzoni Group, 331 Park Avenue South, New York, NY 10010, USA.

Marimekko, Puusepankatu 4, 08810 Helsinki, Finland.

Monkwell, 10–12 Wharfdale Road, Bournemouth, Dorset BH4 9BT, England.

Nobilis-Fontan, 29 rue Bonaparte, 75006 Paris, France and 1–2 Cedar Studios, 45 Glebe Place, London SW3 5JE, England and 1823 Springfield Avenue, New Providence, NJ 07974, USA.

Norlene, San Marco Campo 5, Maurzlo 2606, Venice, Italy.

Les Olivades, Avenue Barberin, 13150, St Etienne-du-Grès, France and 16 Filmer Road, London SW6 7BW, England.

Osborne & Little, 40 Temperley Road, London SW12 8QE, England and 65 Commerce Rd, Stamford, CT 06902, USA.

Pallu & Lake, Unit M27, Chelsea Garden Market, Chelsea Harbour, Lots Road, London SW10 0XE, England.

H A Percheron, 97–99 Cleveland Street, London W1P 5PN, England.

Simon Playle, 6 Fulham Park Studios, Fulham Park Road, London SW6 4LW, England.

Putnam's Collections, 55 Regents Park Road, London NW1 8XD, England.

Arthur Sanderson & Sons, 53 Berners Street, London W1P 3AD, England and Suite 403, 979 Third Avenue, New York, NY 10022, USA.

Schumacher, 979 Third Avenue, New York, NY 10022, USA and through Elizabeth Eaton, 30 Elizabeth Street, London SW1V 9RB, England.

Janet Shand Kydd, The Green Room, 2 Church Street, Framlingham, Suffolk IB13 9BE, England.

Shyam Ahuja, 201 East 56th Street, Third Avenue, New York, NY 10022, USA and through Alton Brook, 5 Sleaford Street, London SW8 5AB, England.

Silk Dynasty, Docey Lewis USA, PO Box 1048, Washington, CT 06703, USA.

Souleiado, 171 Fulham Road, London SW3 6JW, England and through Pierre Deux, 870 Madison Avenue, New York, NY 10014, USA.

Monika Speyer, Wellenburgerstrasse 55, 8900 Augsburg 22, Germany.

Jim Thompson Thai Silk Company, through Mary Fox Linton, 249 Fulham Road, London SW3 6HY, England and through Rodolph, 999 West Spain Street, PO Box 1249, Sonoma, CA 95476, USA.

Bernard Thorp & Company, 6 Burnsall Street, London SW3 3SR, England.

Timney Fowler, 388 Kings Road, London SW3 5UZ, England.

Tissunique, 58–60 Berners St, London W1P 3AE, England.

Warner Fabrics, 7–11 Noel Street, London W1V 4AL, England and through Greeff Fabrics, 150 Midland Avenue, Port Chester, NY 10573, USA.

Watts & Company, 7 Tufton Street, London SW1P 3QE, England and through Christopher Hyland, Suite 1714, 979 Third Avenue, New York, NY 10022, USA.

Zoffany, 63 South Audley Street, London W1Y 5BF, England and through Christopher Hyland, Suite 1714, 979 Third Avenue, New York, NY 10022, USA.

Zuber & Cie, 28 rue Zuber, 68170 Rixheim, France.

CHRONOLOGICAL TABLE

2000 BC Silk weaving originates in China.

1800–700 BC Tapestries of legendary splendour woven by Babylonians and Assyrians (no examples found).

1500–1400 BC Earliest surviving examples of tapestries woven in Egypt.

400–300 BC Block printing first developed in Far East.

206 BC–AD 220 Silk brocades woven in China under Han Dynasty.

300–700 Narrative tapestries woven in Egypt by Copts.

500 Peruvian tapestries and double-cloths in bright-coloured wools first woven, beginning a tradition lasting over a thousand years.

500–600 Wool tapestries and figured silks woven in Persia under Sassanian dynasty.

500s–700s Silks woven in imperial palaces of Byzantium.

600s Silk tapestries, sometimes incorporating metallic threads, first woven in China under T'ang Dynasty.

800s Earliest examples of printed fabrics buried in Coptic tombs at Panapolis; examples of fabrics printed between then and thirteenth century are scarce.

800s Sicilian weavers at Palermo begin to turn out silks with Islamic patterns.

800s Tapestry weaving established in Flanders; industry thrives for nine hundred years.

960–1279 Brocades woven in China under Sung Dynasty.

1100s Italian silk-weaving industry is established, first in Lucca then in Genoa, Venice and Florence, and dominates European market for over four centuries.

1200s India begins producing fine printed fabrics depicting natural forms of flora, with uninhibited use of colour.

1300–early 1400s Paris and the Flemish city of Arras are the two main centres of European tapestry weaving.

Early 1400s Earliest surviving examples of European wallpaper produced.

Mid 1400s Silk-weaving established in Britain.

Mid to late 1400s Flemish cities of Tournai and Brussels are the two main centres of European tapestry weaving.

Late 1400s French silk-weaving established; within two and a half centuries, Lyon is the centre of European silk production.

Late 1400s–early 1500s Japanese tapestry weaving developed from Chinese techniques.

1500s Persia, reconstituted as a nation, produces silk brocades, reaching an artistic peak at the end of the sixteenth century, though they were known and valued by the West before then.

c. 1500 Discovery of Golden House of Nero, revealing a wealth of ornament from ancient Rome.

1509 Earliest known British wallpaper produced.

1500s–1600s Under Mogul dynasty in India, fine cotton "muslins" and woven cashmeres are produced bearing "pine" motif and other floral forms, often richly brocaded with gold.

1500s–1600s Simple block-printed lining papers and wallpapers produced in Europe.

1500s–1600s Non-colourfast printed linen and cotton produced in Britain and on the Continent.

1560s First English tapestry manufactory set up by William Sheldon in Warwickshire.

1600s Aubusson, Gobelins and Beauvais, all in France, and Brussels are the main European centres of tapestry production.

1600s Indian calicoes first imported to Europe by the East India Companies.

1619 James I of England founds the Mortlake manufactory for tapestry weaving; it thrives until the 1680s.

1650s First European workshops to produce imitation Indian calicoes set up in Marseilles. Shortly after, other British and Continental printworks are set up for the same purpose.

late 1600s French Huguenot refugees establish silk-weaving centres in Britain, Ireland, the Netherlands, Germany and Switzerland. London's Spitalfields becomes a major European centre for fine silk damasks and brocades.

c. 1680 Flock wallpaper introduced in England imitating imported Genoa velvet; it reaches the peak of its popularity between about 1715 and 1745.

1680s–1690s Hand-painted Chinese wallpapers introduced into Europe; in large, non-repeating designs, the papers become highly fashionable between about 1740 and 1790.

1700s European chinoiserie papers, in imitation of the Chinese wallpapers, are produced; they are initially hand-drawn and hand-coloured, but later block-printed.

1733 Invention of the "flying shuttle", little used at first but later contributing to the beginning of the Industrial Revolution, which starts in the textile industry.

1740s John Baptist Jackson pioneers oil-based colours and chiaroscuro techniques for printing wallpapers, producing his best work in the 1750s and 1760s.

1740s Excavations at Pompeii and Herculaneum reveal Roman styles of architecture and decoration.

1740s Horace Walpole converts his home Strawberry Hill, near London, in the Gothic manner, creating a model for the new Gothick fashion.

1746 The first print works at Mulhouse, in Alsace, begins printing cottons in imitation of Indian calicoes, introducing block printing with the use of mordants in 1748.

1750–1800 Print rooms become popular in England, featuring walls decorated with prints framed in paper borders and with other paper decorations in Neoclassical style.

1750s–1760s Copperplate printing of furnishing fabrics (including single-colour cotton "toiles") begun in Ireland and London; printing of wallpapers by copper plate (for subsequent hand-colouring) also attempted.

1760s and 1770s Invention of the spinning jenny and "mule", enabling high-speed cotton spinning and contributing to the Industrial Revolution.

1764 Wallpaper first printed by hand-operated cylinders, though actual manufacture does not begin until the 1830s.

1765 First American wallpaper factory opens in New York.

1770 Single-colour copperplate-printed cottons (*toiles de Jouy*) first produced by the brothers Oberkampf at their factory in Jouy-en-Josas, France, and subsequently exported to Britain and America.

1770–1789 The French firm of Réveillon produces Neoclassical wallpapers.

Late 1700s Woven woollen shawls imported into England and the Continent from India.

1780 British weavers from Norwich, Edinburgh and London Spitalfields begin producing imitations of the Indian shawls; Paisley in Scotland follows suit a little later, becoming a major producer in the nineteenth century and giving its name to the paisley pattern. In Europe, Lyon and Vienna become major centres of "paisley" weaving in the nineteenth century, and printed versions are produced in Europe and America.

1780s and 1790s Roller printing of fabrics introduced in Lancashire, England and Jouy, France.

1793 Eli Whitney perfects the cotton gin, opening the door to mass production in the cotton industry.

Late 1700s–1850 Large-scale scenic wallpapers produced in France and exported to America in particular.

Early 1800s Jacquard loom perfected in France by Joseph-Marie Jacquard; introduced into Britain and America twenty years later.

1810 First American silk factory is built, in Mansfield, Connecticut.

1815–1821 The Royal Pavilion at Brighton, England transformed by John Nash, J G Crace and Robert Jones into the ultimate in chinoiserie.

1830s Roller printing of fabrics begins to take the place of copper-plate printing and block-printing.

1830s Continuous paper becomes available, enabling wallpaper to be produced in rolls. Wallpaper is manufactured for the first time on roller-printing machines adapted from the textile industry. The age of mass production is underway.

1844 First wallpaper printing machine imported into the United States.

1851 Great Exhibition at Crystal Palace in London's Hyde Park, where many countries' manufacturers and designers show wallpapers and fabrics.

1856 W H Perkin prepares first aniline dye—mauvine—from coal tar; other colours soon follow.

1861 Firm of Morris, Marshall, Faulkner & Company set up by William Morris.

1860s and 1870s 1862 International Exhibition triggers off a fashion for Japanese decoration, culminating in the Aesthetic movement.

1871 Washable "sanatory papers" introduced.

1875 Arthur Liberty opens his shop in London's Regent Street.

1875 Walter Crane begins designing nursery papers; other artists, such as Kate Greenaway and Mabel Lucy Attwell, follow suit.

1876 The Philadelphia Centennial Exhibition helps foster an interest in Colonial and Federal styles of decoration and also in medieval crafts.

1879 The decorating firm Associated Artists is founded in the United States by Louis C Tiffany, Candace Wheeler, Samuel Colman and Lockwood de Forest. Four years later it becomes a supplier of textiles, wallpapers and embroideries.

1880 The Silver Studio is founded in Britain by Arthur Silver.

1888 Arts and Crafts Exhibition Society launched by William Morris.

1895–1905 Art Nouveau style flourishes on Continent. In Britain it is developed principally by Charles Rennie Mackintosh and the Glasgow School, and in the United States by Louis C Tiffany.

1895–1910 Wallpaper friezes produced by William Shand Kydd, and also by the

Silver Studio and such artists as Lindsay Butterfield, Walter Crane and William Neatby.

Late 1800s Embossed and gilded leather-effect wallpapers produced.

1892 Viscose rayon invented in England.

1899 Wallpaper Manufacturers Ltd formed in England.

Early 1900s Hand silk-screen printing introduced.

1913 Omega Workshop formed by Roger Fry, Vanessa Bell and Duncan Grant; disbands seven years later.

1919 Bauhaus founded in Germany by Walter Gropius; closed 1933.

Early 1920s Constructivist textile patterns created by Russian artists.

1925 Exposition Internationale des Arts Décoratifs et Industriels Modernes in Paris launches Art Deco as a populist style.

1933 Dorland Hall, London, exhibition launches modern style in Britain.

1930s Hand silk-screen printing developed commercially in France, Britain and the United States.

1940 First Museum of Modern Art (New York) "Good Design" exhibition.

1951 Festival of Britain features fabrics with patterns based on molecular structure of crystals, influencing textile design in the 1950s.

1951 John Line's "Limited Editions" are Britain's first screen-printed wallpapers.

1950s Screen printing increasingly used for textiles and wallpapers.

1953 Exhibition "Painting into Textiles" staged by the Institute of Contemporary Art in England.

1956 Reactive dyes introduced for cotton and acetate printing.

1960s Photogravure used for printing some wallpapers.

1960s Development of galvano screen for screen-printing, which becomes increasingly mechanized.

1976 American Bicentenary launches "Americana" fashions in decoration.

1989 French Bicentenary brings document toile patterns and French neo-classical styles into wallpaper and textile ranges.

1980s–1990s Computerization of Jacquard loom enables production of damasks, brocades and tapestries in enormous range of patterns and colourways.

GLOSSARY

ACANTHUS A stylized representation of the jagged leaf of the acanthus plant as in the Corinthian capital of Classical architecture. The most common of all Classical motifs, it

was in almost continuous use from the fifth century BC in Greece until the nineteenth century in the West. Greek and Byzantine designs incorporated a stiffer, more formal acanthus leaf than Roman and Renaissance designs.

ACETATE See Viscose.

ALENTOURS A type of tapestry (qv) in which a central subject resembling a framed painting was surrounded by ornamental motifs; woven at the Gobelins factory near Paris in the eighteenth century.

ANTHEMION A stylized flower motif commonly found in Classical ornament. Consisting of a number of radiating petals,

it was developed by the ancient Greeks from the honeysuckle or lotus palmette motif of ancient Egypt and Asia.

ARABESQUE A type of decoration characterized by symmetrical intertwining branches, leaves and other plant forms, together with abstract curvilinear shapes. The arabesque was originally devised by Hellenistic craftsmen working in Asia Minor, and was adapted by Muslim artists around AD 1000, becoming a traditional part of Islamic decoration. It was used in Europe from the early Renaissance, after arabesques were found in Roman tombs. Raphael used the motif in the decoration of the loggia, or open galleries, of the Vatican. Renaissance arabesques included human beings, beasts and birds (all forbidden in Islamic designs) as well as

flowers, with much interlacing of vines, ribbons and other sinuous shapes. They fell out of fashion during the Baroque period, but the discovery of Roman arabesques at Herculaneum in the mid-eighteenth century brought them back into favour until the early nineteenth century.

ART DECO A style of design fashionable in the 1920s and 1930s, characterized by solid rectilinear shapes and geometric and stylized motifs. In its purest form reliant on expensive, exotic materials.

ART NOUVEAU A decorative art style of the late nineteenth century with an emphasis on sinuous, flowing lines; in the work of Charles Rennie Mackintosh and the Glasgow School there was also a strong vertical element.

ARTS AND CRAFTS A movement led by William Morris in the late nineteenth century dedicated to bringing back into the home the high standards of craftsmanship and design common in the Middle Ages. The movement took its name from the Arts and Crafts Exhibition Society, launched in 1888 by Morris and others.

ASTER A very early motif taking its form from the daisy.

BATIK A fabric patterned by the batik method of resist-dyeing, in which liquid wax or a similar substance is applied to the fabric so that those parts will not take up the dye.

BLOCK PRINTING Hand printing using wooden blocks which have been carved to leave a raised area; this is covered in dye and pressed on to the fabric or paper. It was the major form of printing until the mid-eighteenth century.

BROCADE A damask-based fabric in which short lengths of colour—often gold or silver—are added by small shuttles and turned back at the motif's edge, not being used where not required, rather like embroidery. Today it can also refer to a rich, heavy Jacquard weave in which the pattern is emphasized by contrasting colours and textures. Brocade may be produced in any fibre.

BROCATELLE Similar to damask (qv), a brocatelle weave normally has a satin or

twill pattern on a plain or satin ground. Because it contains a double warp, some areas appear raised. It normally has a silk warp and a cotton, linen or jute weft. It is usually in one colour.

CALICO Originally, a printed and painted cotton first imported from Calico in India and later also manufactured in Britain, the Continent and the United States. In Britain the term now means a coarse, unprinted white cotton, either bleached or unbleached, and in the United States a sturdy printed cotton.

CARTOUCHE Ornament in scroll form, with rolled up ends, such as the elaborate frames

around tablets or coats of arms; also refers to an oval shape enclosing Egyptian hieroglyphs.

CHENILLE Yarn or fabric with a soft velvety pile. Modern chenille may be cotton, viscose, wool or mixtures.

CHIAROSCURO Use of light and shade to create a three-dimensional effect. The chiaroscuro printing technique for wallpapers, using monochrome wood blocks, was first developed by John Baptist Jackson, who had studied the work of the Italian Renaissance chiaroscuro engravers.

CHINOISERIE The use of imitation Chinese motifs in Western interior decoration and furnishings, which became popular in the eighteenth century. Influences from China, India and Japan were often mingled.

CHINTZ A cotton fabric, usually glazed, patterned with flowers, fruit and birds, and printed in several colours, often on a light ground. The term derived from the Hindu word meaning "spotted cloth", referring to the original imported Indian calico (qv).

CLASSICAL Adhering to ancient Greek and Roman models, which were based on mathematical laws of proportion. The Classical style has been the predominant style of Western civilization since the fifth century BC, particularly during the Renaissance and the Neoclassical revivals of the eighteenth and nineteenth centuries.

COPPER-PLATE PRINTING Printing from an engraved copper plate, which was perfected in the eighteenth century. Today the best-known fabrics printed by this method were the *toiles de Jouy* (qv). In the 18th century the French called them *toiles d'Ireland*, after the site of their early production.

COTTON The fibres covering the boll of the cotton plant, or thread or cloth made from these fibres.

CYLINDER PRINTING A type of machine printing using engraved metal rollers to print wallpapers. A very similar method, roller printing (qv), was developed for printing fabric.

DADO The part of an interior wall beneath the chair rail. Derived from a Classical order, it corresponds to the pedestal, or dado, on which a column is supported, with the chair rail corresponding to the cornice of the pedestal and the skirting board to the base. The infill (also called "filling"), or area of the wall between the picture and chair rails, corresponds to the column itself and the frieze (qv) to the entablature resting on the column.

DAMASK A compound-weave fabric, in which the pattern is created by the contrasting textures of the glossy satin-weave (qv) ground and the matt sateen-weave (qv) motifs. Woven on Jacquard looms since the nineteenth century, damask generally features large or elaborate patterns and is usually reversible. It takes its name from the Syrian capital of Damascus, which was one of the main centres of the silk trade. Traditionally silk or linen, damask can also be woven from cotton, wool or a mixture of fibres. In a single damask, the satin weave is tied down by every fifth weft, while in a double damask it is tied down at every eighth weft, creating a tighter, more lustrous texture.

DAMASQUETTE A type of lampas (qv). It is similar to damask (qv) but with an additional single-coloured warp which usually matches the weft, creating solid-coloured areas where the two cross.

DIAPER A repeat pattern composed of lozenge (qv) or square shapes, usually

based on a diamond grid, each of which may contain a flower, spray of leaves or similar motif.

DISCHARGE PRINTING A method of hand-printing a dyed fabric with a bleaching agent to leave areas of white. Sometimes a bleach-resistant dye is added to the bleaching agent to create coloured areas rather than white, a technique developed soon after 1800 and then called "lapis".

DOBBY Small, all-over, geometric pattern woven on a dobby loom.

DOCUMENT FABRICS/PAPERS Faithful reproductions of textiles and wallpapers from the past, many of which use the original dyes and printing techniques.

DOUBLE-CLOTH A large group of fabrics, the most common being a strong, reversible fabric consisting of two separate cloths, each with its own warp and weft, which are interwoven.

FESTOON A decoration representing a garland (qv) tied together with ribbons and suspended between two points so that it drapes in the middle. The ends are sometimes held by bulls, lions or other animals, or they may be tied into bows

with the ends of the ribbons hanging down. Widely used in Classical ornamentation, it is also often known as a swag, though sometimes "swag" is used to mean a festoon made of folds of cloth.

FIGURED WEAVE Patterned by the weave structure, as in figured silks or velvets.

FLEUR DE LYS Small floral ornament and heraldic device. Originally based on the lily, it is composed of three petals bound

together near the base. The name is from the French for "flower of the lily" and it was the former royal arms of France.

FLOCK A technique for patterning wallpaper to make it look like velvet or damask, achieved by applying glue to the paper and then sprinkling (originally) or spraying (today) powdered fibres over it.

FRET An ornamental pattern composed of

straight lines, usually joined at right angles, within a border. Also called Greek key.

FRIEZE The upper portion of an interior wall, between the cornice and the picture rail. Also used to describe wallpapers manufactured especially for this part of the wall. Derived from a Classical order, the frieze corresponds to the flat central section of an entablature, which rests on a column. The cornice corresponds to the cornice of the entablature, and the picture rail to the architrave of the entablature. The infill, or area of the wall between the picture and chair rails, corresponds to the column itself, and the dado (qv) to the pedestal supporting the column.

FYLFOT A key or swastika pattern.

GARLAND A Classical motif depicting a chain of flowers and foliage, which may be joined at the ends to form a wreath, or draped in loops to form a festoon (qv).

GENOA VELVET A velvet (qv) patterned during weaving, with a multicoloured pile and a satin ground. Originally the term meant silk-brocaded velvets with a satin ground, hand woven in Genoa.

GINGHAM Broadly, a striped or checked plain-woven cotton cloth made from dyed yarns, as produced in the nineteenth century. However, the term is usually used in a narrower sense, to mean a cotton cloth with balanced (equal-width) checks, woven from two colours (one normally white), so that a darker colour is formed where the two stripes cross.

GOTHIC A style of architecture and design which dominated western Europe between the twelfth and sixteenth centuries and was characterized by pointed arches, ribbed vaults, intricate window tracery and an emphasis on vertical lines. Revivals of the style in the eighteenth and nineteenth centuries were sometimes known as Gothick, Gothic Revival or Neo-Gothic.

GRISAILLE Monochromatic painting in shades of grey in imitation of bas-reliefs.

GROTESQUE Ornamental motif based on Roman ornament found in a "grotto" (underground chamber containing murals) c. 1500 in the Golden House of Nero. Extravagantly formed, they included human and animal figures some of which terminated in coiling foliage, combined with floral and foliate ornament and arabesques (qv). Raphael used grotesques for the decoration of the loggia, or open galleries, of the Vatican, and they were widely used until the late eighteenth century. Tapestries known as grotesques, which featured this type of ornamentation, were produced at Beauvais in France in the late seventeenth century.

IKAT A fabric patterned by the ikat method of resist-dyeing, in which strands of yarn are bound tightly together at chosen intervals and dyed, then untied, rebound in different places and dyed with a second colour, and so on. The dye does not take where the yarn has been bound, thereby creating a pattern. The dyed yarns are then woven in particular designs, which have a characteristically fuzzy outline. First developed in Indonesia.

ISLAND PATTERN Pattern in which the motif is isolated in repeat on a plain background.

JACQUARD A loom invented by a Frenchman, Joseph-Marie Jacquard, at the beginning of the nineteenth century. It used perforated cards to control the pattern, enabling complicated figured fabrics to be woven. Sophisticated computerized versions of this loom are used today to produce very complex, richly patterned and coloured weaves.

KASURI Japanese type of weaving using resist-dyeing techniques.

KENTE CLOTH A type of cloth made in Africa by joining narrow strips of woven cloth to form bold, graphic patterns. Many have been woven in silk, or silk and cotton, to be worn by chiefs.

KILIM The modern descendant of the Persian tapestry, the kilim is a pileless ethnic rug usually woven by the slit-tapestry technique, which is characterized by narrow slits between blocks of colour. Woven in India (where it is known as a dhurrie), the Near East and eastern Europe, kilims are most often made from wool but sometimes from cotton or silk, in boldly coloured, simple geometric patterns.

LAMPAS A compound-weave fabric similar to damask (qv) with areas of unblended colour, created by using extra warps or wefts in the patterned areas. Damasquette, lisère and tissue (qqv) are all lampas.

LINEN Fabric woven from flax yarns, spun from the fibres of the flax plant.

LISÈRE A type of lampas (qv) with a striped additional warp.

LOTUS Ornamental motif based on the waterlily of the Nile, which appeared in ancient Egyptian decoration.

LOZENGE A rhombus-shaped motif.

MEDALLION A rounded ornament often containing other motifs.

MILLEFLEURS TAPESTRY A type of tapestry (qv) characterized by tiny flowers used as a background to a larger design, usually a secular or allegorical scene. Produced in many parts of France, particularly the Loire valley, and the Low Countries in the fifteenth and sixteenth centuries.

MOIRÉ A watered finish (qv), creating a wavelike pattern by pressing a design on to a ribbed fabric using high-pressure engraved rollers.

MORDANT A substance, particularly a metal salt such as alum, which combines with the cloth and the dyestuff, making the dyed fabric colourfast.

MOREEN A stout cotton, wool or worsted weave, usually with a stamped or watered finish (qv) in imitation of damask (qv).

OGEE A shape usually formed by two continuous confronting concave and

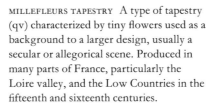

convex curves, similar to the letter S; often used in Islamic designs in particular.

OGIVAL In the shape of an ogee (qv).

PAISLEY A printed or woven design derived from woven shawls originally imported from India, and subsequently produced in Paisley, Scotland, as well as a number of other British and Continental locations. It is characterized by rich, curvilinear, highly stylized floral forms and particularly a motif shaped rather like a large comma, all derived from the Mogul art of India.

PALAMPORE An Indian bedcover made from colourful hand-painted Indian calico (qv).

PALM A palm-shaped divided-leaf motif.

PALMETTE A conventionalized palm leaf motif, resembling a spread fan.

PASTICHE A composition such as a picture in the style of one or more other artists.

PLUSH A cut-pile fabric similar to velvet but with a longer, less dense pile.

POLYESTER A man-made fibre produced from the by-products of petrol refining. Polyester has made it possible to create strong though apparently delicate weaves. It is often combined with natural fibres such as cotton.

POLYGON A many-sided figure, used in many Chinese and Japanese designs.

PROVENÇAL PRINT A bright, multicoloured cotton print with a small but predominant pattern, whether floral, geometric or paisley (qv), produced in the South of France.

QUATREFOIL A leaf motif having four foils,

or lobes; very typical of Gothic ornamentation.

RAYON See Viscose.

REP A horizontally ribbed weave using thick and fine yarns together to create the ribbed effect. Woven from wool, silk, rayon or cotton.

RESIST DYEING Various methods of creating pattern by tying up the yarn or fabric tightly, or treating the fabric with a substance such as wax or starch paste, prior to dyeing so that the dye cannot reach the treated areas. Batik and ikat (qqv) are two types of resist dyeing.

ROCAILLE An ornamental style of the eighteenth century employing stylized pebble and shell shapes and scrolls. (*Rocaille* is the French word for pebbles.) Asymmetrical and featuring single and double curves, it was very typical of Rococo decoration; in fact, in France *style rocaille* is synonymous with Rococo (qv). When the Rouen potters adopted *rocaille* ornamentation, this in turn influenced the patterning of silks woven in Lyon during the eighteenth century.

ROCOCO A style of decoration popular in eighteenth-century Europe, particularly in France, where it originated. It was characterized by light and delicate, asymmetrical ornament, with swirling motifs including shellwork, foliage and S-shaped curves, and also much chinoiserie (qv). Revived in the second half of the nineteenth century.

ROLLER PRINTING A type of continuous machine printing using engraved metal rollers to print long lengths of cloth. A very similar method, cylinder printing (qv), was developed for printing wallpaper.

ROSETTE Motif of a knot of radiating loops of ribbons arranged concentrically, or closely radiating groups of leaves.

ROUNDEL A small, decorative type of medallion (qv).

SATEEN The back of a satin weave (qv),

with a matt surface, which is used for the figured area in damask (qv); also refers to cotton satin.

SATIN A simple weave in which the warp and weft threads are interlaced in an apparently random order, creating a glossy surface because the weft threads are almost completely hidden by the fine, close-set warp. Satin weave is used for the ground in damask (qv) and although any fibre can be used, is usually made from silk or rayon (qqv).

SCANDINAVIAN MODERN The Scandinavian twentieth century Arts and Crafts (qv) style, in which traditional techniques and craftsman-made furnishings blended with modern needs. It was typified by informality and fresh colours.

SCENIC PAPER French nineteenth-century block-printed wallpaper designed to run around all four walls of a room, forming a continuous panorama. It was very popular in America as well as in France.

SCREEN PRINTING A printing process similar to stencilling, with colourant forced through a prepared screen of fine mesh. Rotary screen printing is used to print most fabrics and wallpapers today.

SILK The fibres produced by the larvae of the silk moth, or thread or cloth made from these fibres.

STRAPWORK Decoration of interlaced fillets resembling leather straps. It developed from the flat scrolls used in Islamic metalwork and was much used during the sixteenth and seventeenth centuries. It was also popular in eighteenth-century French decoration, and it appeared in nineteenth-century textiles that emulated Renaissance styles.

SWAG See Festoon.

SYNTHETIC FIBRES A large group of fibres made by grouping chemical compounds, mainly from the petroleum group. They include nylon, polyester, acrylic and vinyl; the term is not applicable to acetate, viscose (qv) or their generic, rayon.

TAFFETA A crisp, smooth, closely woven plain-weave fabric traditionally made from silk (qv) but today also made from silk-like fabrics such as rayon.

TAPESTRY A hand-woven decorative fabric in which the design is built up during the weaving process; also the term for the weaving technique itself. The weft threads are not carried the full width of the fabric but woven in where each is used in the design. The weft completely covers the warp, and the fabric is reversible. From the mid-nineteenth century the term has also included machine-woven tapestries, which are warp-faced (qv) and are not reversible.

TEAR PENDANT A motif looking like a teardrop, as used in Peruvian weaving.

TISSUE A type of lampas (qv) with extra colouring wefts, simulating hand brocading.

TOILE DE JOUY A cotton fabric printed with pictorial scenes, usually in a single colour on an off-white ground. Originally the term referred to the copperplate-printed cottons from the Oberkampf factory at Jouy-en-Josas, in France, which were produced from 1770, but today "toile" indicates any fabric of this type.

TREFOIL A leaf motif having three foils, or

lobes; very typical of Gothic ornamentation.

TROMPE L'OEIL Images which "deceive the eye" by creating the illusion of three dimensions, suggesting that the image is real. The technique was used by the Greeks and Romans and was also employed during the early Renaissance, as well as in Neoclassical revivals of the eighteenth, nineteenth and twentieth centuries.

TURKEYWORK Using knots to imitate the effect of rugs from the Near East.

TURKISH CORNER An area of a room, such as an inglenook or large bay, decorated and furnished with Near Eastern textiles. Shawls, kilims (qv), and fabrics such as Ottoman velvets (patterned with ogees or pomegranates) were used to cover window seats or other built-in seating, Turkish divans or daybeds, and cushions. Draperies and embroidered throws were also used. Popular at the end of the nineteenth century.

TWILL A simple weave in which the warp and weft threads are interlaced in steps to form diagonal twill lines on the surface.

UTRECHT VELVET A cut-pile fabric, traditionally mohair on linen, in which a pattern is created by crushing areas of the pile using heated engraved rollers.

VELVET A fabric with a thick, soft pile, made from the warp threads. A wide range of fibres may be used for velvet, including silk, cotton, wool, viscose or a mixture. Usually the pile is cut, but terry velvet has an uncut pile. Genoa velvet and Utrecht velvet (qqv) are both patterned.

VELVETEEN A cotton velvet with a pile made from the weft, rather than the warp as in velvet (qv).

VERDURE TAPESTRY A type of tapestry (qv), also known as garden tapestry, in which the design was based on plant forms and foliage. Landscapes were also incorporated in the later *verdure* tapestries. They were produced in the sixteenth and seventeenth centuries in France, and the tapestry workshop at Aubusson specialized in them. Many were small and were used for upholstery or as cushion covers.

VISCOSE A man-made fibre made from cellulose (usually wood pulp), and spun like conventional fibres (and called rayon "staple" yarn) or, more recently, extruded as in silk-making. Rayon was formerly also the generic term for acetate, also from a cellulose compound, which is extruded.

VOLUTE A deep spiral scroll or spiral shell motif, which appears in Ionic capitals of

Classical architecture. Its name refers to its resemblance to the marine snail known as the volute.

WARP The lengthwise threads in a loom. Also known as the "ends", they are placed under tension, and the weft (qv) threads are interlaced over and under them.

WARP-FACED A textile in which a large proportion of the warp threads are on the surface, hiding the weft.

WATERED FINISH Wavy patterns on a fabric, such as a watered silk, which look like water marks. They are made by passing a ribbed fabric through high-pressure engraved cylinders.

WEFT The crosswise threads in a loom. Also known as the "picks", they are interlaced over and under the warp (qv) threads.

WEFT-FACED A textile in which a large proportion of the weft threads are on the surface, hiding the warp.

WOOL The fibres produced from animal fleece, usually sheep or goat, or yarn or cloth made from these fibres.

WORSTED The firmly twisted yarn or thread spun from combed wool, which is smoother than carded wool, or the fabric woven from this.

BIBLIOGRAPHY

Artley, Alexandra (editor), *Putting Back the Style*, Swallow Publishing Ltd for Evans Brothers Ltd, 1982.

Bargert, Albrecht and Armer, Karl Michael, *'80s Style—Designs of the Decade*, Thames & Hudson, 1990.

Bayley, Stephen (editor), *The Conran Directory of Design*, Conran Octopus, 1985.

Birren, Faber, *Colour*, Mitchell Beazley (A Marshall Edition), 1980.

Brédif, Josette, *Toiles de Jouy, Classic Printed Textiles from France 1760–1843*, Thames & Hudson, 1989.

Bury, H, *A Choice of Design 1850–1980—Fabrics by Warner & Sons Ltd*, Warners, 1981.

Dupont-Auberville, M, *Classic Textile Designs* (Ducher et Cie, 1977), Bracken Books, 1989.

Glazier, R, *Historic Textile Fabrics*, B T Batsford, 1923.

Gore, Alan and Ann, *The History of English Interiors*, Phaidon Press Ltd, 1991.

Hamilton, Jean, *An Introduction to Wallpaper*, Her Majesty's Stationery Office, 1983.

Hecht, Ann, *The Art of the Loom*, British Museum Publications, 1989.

Jones, Owen, *The Grammar of Ornament*, 1856. New edition, Studio Editions, 1986.

Joseph, Marjory L, *Introductory Textile Science*, Holt, Reinhart & Winston, 1972.

Larsen, Jack Lenor, *Furnishing Fabrics, an International Sourcebook*, Thames & Hudson, 1989.

Lubell, Cecil, *Textile Collections of the World* (3 volumes), Studio Vista, c. 1976.

Lynn, Catherine, *Wallpaper in America*, W W Norton & Company, 1980.

MacCarthy, Fiona, *British Design Since 1880*, Lund Humphries, 1982.

Miller, Judith and Martin, *Period Style*, Mitchell Beazley International Ltd, 1989.

Oman, Charles C and Hamilton, Jean, *Wallpapers—a History and Illustrated Catalogue of the Collection in the Victoria and Albert Museum*, Philip Wilson Publishers for Sotheby Publications in association with the Victoria & Albert Museum, 1982.

The Omega Workshops 1913–1919, Crafts Council, 1984.

Paine, Melanie, *Textile Classics*, Mitchell Beazley, 1990.

Parry, Linda, *Textiles of the Arts and Crafts Movement*, Thames & Hudson, 1988.

Parry, Linda, *William Morris and The Arts & Crafts Movement*, Studio Vista, 1989.

Picton, John, and Mack, John, *African Textiles*, British Museum Publications, 1979.

Reilly, Valerie, *Paisley Patterns*, Studio Editions, 1989.

Rothstein, Natalie, *Eighteenth Century Silk Designs*, Thames & Hudson, 1990.

Safford, Carleton L and Bishop, Robert, *America's Quilts and Coverlets*, Studio Vista, 1974.

Schoeser, Mary, *Fabrics and Wallpapers*, Bell & Hyman, 1986.

Schoeser, Mary, *French Textiles 1760 to the present*, Calmann & King, 1991.

Schoeser, Mary, *Marianne Straub*, Design Council, 1984.

Schoeser, Mary, *Owen Jones Silks*, Warner Fabrics plc, 1987.

Schoeser, Mary and Rufey, Celia, *English and American Textiles from 1790 to the Present*, Thames & Hudson, 1989.

Tomlin, Julian (editor), *The Whitworth Art Gallery, The First Hundred Years*, Whitworth Art Gallery, 1988.

Turner, Mark and Hoskins, Lesley, *Silver Studio of Design*, Webb & Bower, 1988.

Wells-Cole, Anthony, *Historic Paper Hangings from Temple Newsam and Other English Houses*, Leeds City Art Galleries, 1983.

Yasinskaya, I, *Soviet Textile Designs of the Revolutionary Period*, Thames & Hudson, 1990.

INDEX

〜